이화 한국어

참고서

STUDY GUIDE

이화여자대학교 언어교육원
Ewha Womans University
Ewha Language Center

이화 한국어

참고서

박진철 · 이소연 · 이승은 지음

English Version

3-2

EPRESS

이화 한국어 참고서 3-2 (English Version)

지은이 박진철 · 이소연 · 이승은

펴낸날 초판 1쇄 2016년 3월 4일
펴낸이 김훈순 **펴낸곳** 이화여자대학교출판문화원
주소 서울특별시 서대문구 이화여대길 52(우 03760) **등록** 1954년 7월 6일 제9-61호
전화 02) 3277-2965(편집), 02) 362-6076(마케팅)
팩스 02) 312-4312 **전자우편** press@ewha.ac.kr **홈페이지** www.ewhapress.com

번역 최윤영 · 조윤정 **감수** 홍영예 **진행** 김현진 · 정누리
책임편집 이혜지 **디자인** 김리영 **인쇄** 한영문화사

ISBN 979-11-5890-148-6 18710
978-89-7300-875-9 (세트)
값 10,000원

* 잘못된 책은 바꾸어 드립니다.

» Contents

Table of Contents

G Grammar V&E Vocabulary & Expression S Script D Dialogue RG Reading Guide TV Topic Vocabulary Tell Tell me!

Contents

Part2		Part3		Vocabulary Check
들어 봅시다	말해 봅시다	읽어 봅시다	어휘를 늘려 봅시다	
V&E 흥행작 S Listening to a conversation on arranging to see a performance after hearing about it	V&E 애매하다 / 요기하다 D Passing on a message	V&E 진출하다 / 발걸음을 집으로 향하다 / 입을 다물 수가 없다 RG Grasping the writer's feelings and thoughts from a review	–거리다	TV Performance
V&E 일단 S Listening to a conversation on finding lost items at the subway station's Lost and Found	V&E 책을 몇 권 사다 D Guessing where the item was lost	V&E 제값 / 다음부터는 이런 일이 없기를 바라다 RG Finding out the reason for requesting an exchange from the request letter	–되다	TV Problem Solving
V&E 용 꿈을 꾸다 S Listening to a conversation about conception dreams	V&E 매력에 빠지다 D Talking about unfulfilled dreams	V&E 의미하다 / 영향을 미치다 RG Learning about which dreams are good and which are bad from the explanatory passage	헛–	TV Dream
V&E 사고를 당하다 / 어쨌든 S Listening to a conversation about an accident seen first hand	V&E 자국이 나다 / 엉망이 되다 D Explaining the situation to the police after a robbery	V&E 리본이 달리다 / 평생 / 깜짝 파티를 준비해 놓지 않았을까 하는 기대를 하다 RG Getting to know the author's feelings about a memorable day from a passage written about that day	–받다	TV Accident
V&E 취업난이 심하다 S Listening to a conversation about complaints with the office	V&E 생각이 굴뚝같다 / 월급이 쥐꼬리만 하다 D Talking about one's worries about work	V&E 발 디딜 틈이 없다 / 생각이 스치다 / 배꼽시계가 울리다 / 졸음이 쏟아지다 RG Getting an idea of an office worker's day from the passage	–쟁이	TV Work
V&E 부쩍 늘다 S Listening to a lecture on good interpersonal relations	V&E 말도 마세요 / 도저히 안 될 것 같다 D Refusing a colleague's request	V&E 무심코 한 말 / 상처를 입다 / 이와는 달리 RG Comprehending the standards for classification and types in the passage about classification	얼굴 관련 표현	TV Interpersonal Relationships
V&E 가까운 사이가 되다 S Listening to a presentation on Korean greetings	V&E 일손이 부족하다 D Giving a neighbor information on nearby convenience facilities	V&E 큰절을 올리다 / 입을 맞추다 / 뒤로 물러서다 RG Comprehending the special experiences of the author, who wrote about cultural differences	맨–	TV Life Overseas
V&E 성공담 S Listening to a program about a successful person	V&E 쏜살같이 지나가다 / 일리가 있다 D Persuading a friend who's going to give up studying	V&E 실리다 / 마음을 고쳐먹다 / 패션쇼를 빛내다 RG Comprehending the writer's efforts and future image from the passage sent by the writer to himself/herself	미래 관련 표현	TV Deciding One's Career

How to Use This Book

『이화 한국어 참고서 3-2』 is a study guide for Korean-language learners, accompanying the textbook 『이화 한국어 3-2』. This study guide contains detailed explanation of the grammar, vocabulary and expressions used in the Preparation(준비합시다), Listening(들어 봅시다), Speaking(말해 봅시다), and Reading(읽어 봅시다), Vocabulary Expansion(어휘를 늘려 봅시다) sections of each unit. Additionally, the scripts for the Listening(들어 봅시다) and the dialogues for the Speaking(말해 봅시다) sections have all been translated into English.

준비합시다

Grammar Focus

Grammar points are clearly explained with morphological information in the table below, helping students to understand the usage of grammatical structures and various irregular forms. Adjectives are marked as A, verbs V, and nouns N. In addition, various examples are given to demonstrate grammar in use.

Focus Plus

More detailed explanations of grammar are given such as the constraints of certain forms or differences with other similar grammatical structures, to help students to reduce errors in using grammatical structures.

Answers

Answers to the exercises in the textbook are given. Students can check the correct answers for themselves.

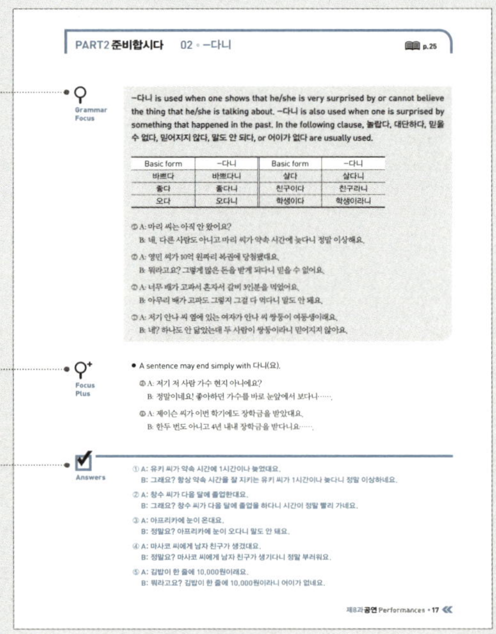

PART2 준비합시다 02 • -다니 p.25

Grammar Focus

-다니 is used when one shows that he/she is very surprised by or cannot believe the thing that he/she is talking about. -다니 is also used when one is surprised by something that happened in the past. In the following clause, 놀랍다, 대단하다, 믿을 수 없다, 믿어지지 않다, 말도 안 되다, or 어이가 없다 are usually used.

Basic form	-다니	Basic form	-다니
바쁘다	바쁘다니	살다	살다니
좋다	좋다니	친구이다	친구라니
오다	오다니	학생이다	학생이라니

A: 마리 씨는 아직 안 왔어요?
B: 네, 다른 사람도 아니고 마리 씨가 약속 시간에 늦다니 정말 이상해요.

A: 영민 씨가 10억 원짜리 복권에 당첨됐대요.
B: 뭐라고요? 그렇게 많은 돈을 받게 되다니 믿을 수 없어요.

A: 너무 배가 고파서 혼자서 갈비 3인분을 먹었어요.
B: 아무리 배가 고파도 그렇지 그걸 다 먹다니 말도 안 돼요.

A: 저기 안나 씨 옆에 있는 여자가 안나 씨 쌍둥이 여동생이래요.
B: 네? 하나도 안 닮았는데 두 사람이 쌍둥이라니 믿어지지 않아요.

Focus Plus

- A sentence may end simply with 다니(요).

A: 저기 저 사람 가수 현지 아니에요?
B: 정말이네요! 좋아하던 가수를 바로 눈앞에서 보다니…….

A: 제이슨 씨가 이번 학기에도 장학금을 받았대요.
B: 한두 번도 아니고 4년 내내 장학금을 받다니요…….

Answers

① A: 유키 씨가 약속 시간에 1시간이나 늦었대요.
B: 그래요? 항상 약속 시간을 잘 지키는 유키 씨가 1시간이나 늦다니 정말 이상하네요.

② A: 창수 씨가 다음 달에 졸업한대요.
B: 그래요? 창수 씨가 다음 달에 졸업을 하다니 시간이 정말 빨리 가네요.

③ A: 아프리카에 눈이 온대요.
B: 정말요? 아프리카에 눈이 오다니 말도 안 돼요.

④ A: 마사코 씨에게 남자 친구가 생겼대요.
B: 정말요? 마사코 씨에게 남자 친구가 생기다니 정말 부러워요.

⑤ A: 김밥이 한 줄에 10,000원이래요.
B: 뭐라고요? 김밥이 한 줄에 10,000원이라니 어이가 없네요.

제8과 공연 Performances • 17

들어 봅시다 / 말해 봅시다 / 읽어 봅시다 / 어휘를 늘려 봅시다

Vocabulary & Expression

Detailed explanations of meaning and usage are given for words and expressions that are useful in daily life. Various examples are given to increase students' understanding.

Script/Dialogue

The text for the Listening(들어 봅시다) and Speaking (말해 봅시다) sections in the textbook have all been translated into English to help students easily understand the contents.

Answers

Answers to the questions in the Listening(들어 봅시다) and Reading(읽어 봅시다) sections are given along with explanations that will help students to confirm their knowledge and understand the contents.

Reading Guide

The types of reading texts are presented to help learners better study the Reading(읽어 봅시다) section, together with a guide to the learning focus.

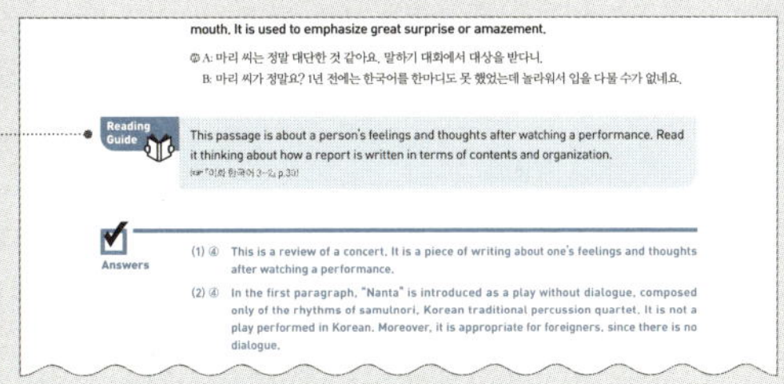

Vocabulary Expansion

Meanings of affixes and collocation introduced in each unit and sample sentences are presented.

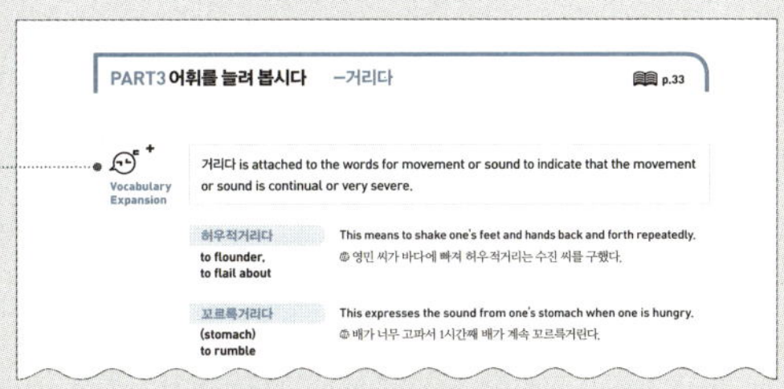

Vocabulary Check

New words listed in the textbook have been translated. Vocabulary words and expressions that are related with the topic of each section are further presented. In addition, new vocabulary words from 『이화 한국어 참고서 3-2』 are listed in the glossary.

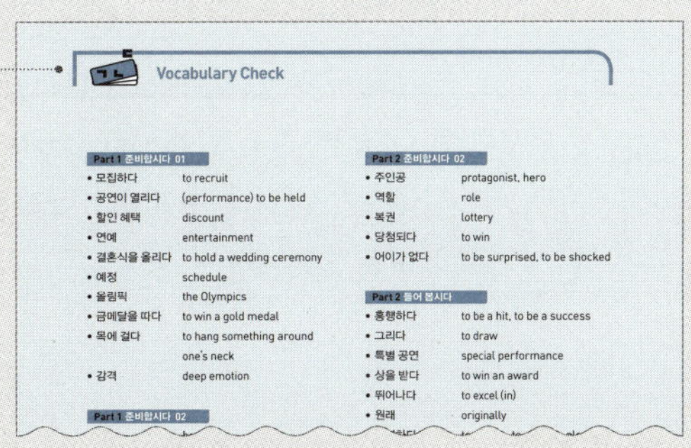

 p.18

Grammar Focus

-ㄴ/는대요 is used when one conveys to another person what he/she has heard from a third party or read. It is an indirect speech contraction of -ㄴ/는다고 하다 and is generally used in spoken language. -대요 is attached to an adjective and -ㄴ/는대요 to a verb. The past tense is -았/었대요 for both verbs and adjectives. -(으)ㄹ 거래요 is used with a verb when one conveys to another person what he/she has heard from a third party or read about something that will happen in the future. On the contrary, -(으)ㄹ 거래요 is used with an adjective when one conveys a guess or assumption that he/she has heard or read about. Nouns are used with (이)래요. 아니다 is changed to 아니래요.

Basic form	-대요	-았/었대요	-(으)ㄹ 거래요
바쁘다	바쁘대요	바빴대요	바쁠 거래요
좋다	좋대요	좋았대요	좋을 거래요
맛있다	맛있대요	맛있었대요	맛있을 거래요
Basic form	-ㄴ/는대요	-았/었대요	-(으)ㄹ 거래요
오다	온대요	왔대요	올 거래요
먹다	먹는대요	먹었대요	먹을 거래요
Basic form	(이)래요	이었/였대요	일 거래요
기자이다	기자래요	기자였대요	기자일 거래요
학생이다	학생이래요	학생이었대요	학생일 거래요

ex A: 제이슨 씨는 아직 안 왔어요? 원래 항상 일찍 오는데 웬일이지요?
B: 안 그래도 방금 전화 왔는데 감기에 걸려서 많이 아프대요. 오늘 못 올 것 같대요.

ex A: 지난주에 개봉한 〈초콜릿〉이라는 영화 봤어요? 정말 재미있대요.
B: 네. 저도 이야기 들었어요. 벌써 10만 명이나 봤대요.

ex A: 어제 TV에서 영화배우 이민형이 자기 이상형을 이야기했다면서요?
B: 네. 이민형은 키가 큰 여자를 좋아한대요. 지난번에 사귀었던 여자 친구도 키가 컸대요.

ex A: 제이슨, 내가 외출한 동안에 마이클한테 전화 왔었지? 뭐래?
B: 다음 주에 미국으로 돌아간대. 가기 전에 한번 만나고 싶대. 자기가 내일 다시 연락하겠대.

ex A: 내일 날씨가 어떨까요?
B: 오늘 아침에 뉴스에서 봤는데 이번 주말까지 계속 추울 거래요.

ex A: 마이클 씨, 유키 씨 부모님이 한국에 오셨다면서요?
B: 네. 유키 씨를 보러 오셨는데 여행도 하고 가실 거래요.

ex A: 안나 씨 남편은 직업이 뭐래요?
B: 기자래요. 독일에 있는 방송국에서 일한대요.

Focus Plus

- A contraction of indirect speech, -ㄴ/는대요 is used when two people have a close relationship with each other. It is not appropriate to use this expression on formal or official occasions.

  ex 곧 회의를 시작하겠습니다. 모두 자리에 앉아 주시기 바랍니다.
  회장님께서는 10분 후에 도착하신다고 합니다. (○)

  ex 곧 회의를 시작하겠습니다. 모두 자리에 앉아 주시기 바랍니다.
  회장님께서는 10분 후에 도착하신대요. (×)

- -ㄴ/는대요 can be used interchangeably with -ㄴ/는댔어요, which is a contraction of -ㄴ/는다고 했어요.

  ex 캐서린 씨가 오늘 밤에 파티에 간다고 해요.
  (= 파티에 간대요)
  (= 파티에 간댔어요)

  ex 캐서린 씨가 어젯밤에 파티에 갔다고 해요.
  (= 파티에 갔대요)
  (= 파티에 갔댔어요)

  ex 캐서린 씨가 내일 밤에 파티에 갈 거라고 해요.
  (= 파티에 갈 거래요)
  (= 파티에 갈 거랬어요)

Answers

① A: 공연 잡지 봤어요?
B: 아니요, 못 봤는데요.
A: 이번 달에 학생들을 위해서 다양한 공연이 열린대요.
학생들에게는 20% 할인 혜택이 있대요.

② A: 인터넷 연예 기사 봤어요?
B: 아니요, 못 봤는데요.
A: 영화배우 김민수 씨와 임희진 씨가 결혼한대요.
결혼식은 이번 겨울쯤에 올릴 예정이래요.

③ A: 텔레비전 스포츠 뉴스 봤어요?
B: 아니요, 못 봤는데요.
A: 이번 올림픽에서 박재범 선수가 금메달을 땄대요.
금메달을 목에 건 순간 박재범 선수는 감격의 눈물을 흘렸대요.

④ A: 신문 생활 정보면 봤어요?
B: 아니요, 못 봤는데요.
A: 요즘 컴퓨터 사용으로 눈이 피로한 사람이 많대요.
눈이 피로할 때는 찬물로 눈을 씻어 주면 좋대요.

Grammar Focus

-기에 is used when one judges a certain behavior or situation using the preceding clause as the basis for judgement. -기에 is attached only to verbs.

Basic form	-기에	Basic form	-기에
가다	가기에	읽다	읽기에
연습하다	연습하기에	걷다	걷기에
먹다	먹기에	살다	살기에

ex A: 유키 씨, 〈무지개〉라는 연극 봤어요? 어때요?
B: 저도 아직 못 봤는데 가족들이 다 같이 보기에 좋은 연극이래요.

ex A: 버스로 이동하는 게 좋을 것 같은데 어떠세요?
B: 우리가 50명이나 되는데 버스 한 대로 이동할 수 있을까요?
모두 한꺼번에 가기에 무리일 것 같아요.

ex A: 손님, 지금 휴가철이라서 작은 방밖에 없어요. 이 방만 남았어요.
B: 네. 그런데 남자 다섯 명이 자기에는 방이 좁네요.

ex A: 이 짐은 흐엉 씨가 혼자 들기엔 좀 무거워 보이네요. 저랑 같이 들어요.
B: 도와줘서 고마워요.

ex A: 종강 파티 때 치킨을 3마리 주문하면 충분하겠지요?
B: 글쎄요. 10명이 먹기에 양이 좀 적은 것 같아요.

ex A: 와, 집이 크고 좋네요. 여기에서 혼자 사세요?
B: 네. 그런데 혼자 살기에는 좀 커서 요즘 룸메이트를 구하고 있어요.

ex A: 이 책은 내용이 좀 어려워서 초등학생들이 읽기에 좀 어려울 것 같아요.
B: 네, 그럴 것 같아요. 중학생은 되어야 읽을 수 있을 것 같네요.

Answers

① A: 피자 한 판을 주문해서 혼자 먹으려고 하는데 괜찮을까요?
B: 글쎄요. 혼자서 먹기에 양이 좀 많아요. 동아리 친구들을 불러서 함께 먹는 게 좋을 것 같아요.

② A: 숙제를 집에 놓고 와서 집에 다시 돌아가려고 하는데 괜찮을까요?
B: 글쎄요. 돌아가기에는 좀 멀리 왔어요. 그냥 다음에 가져오는 게 좋을 것 같아요.

③ A: 급한 일이 있어서 지금 친구에게 전화를 해야 하는데 괜찮을까요?
B: 글쎄요. 지금 친구에게 전화하기에는 시간이 좀 늦었어요. 내일 오전에 하는 게 좋을 것 같아요.

④ A: 이사를 하는데 혼자 이삿짐을 옮기려고 하는데 괜찮을까요?
B: 글쎄요. 혼자 이삿짐을 옮기기에 좀 힘들어요. 이삿짐센터를 부르는 게 좋을 것 같아요.

⑤ A: 10년 동안 다니던 직장을 지금 그만두려고 하는데 괜찮을까요?
B: 글쎄요. 지금 그만두기에는 좀 아까워요. 조금 더 다니면서 다른 직장을 알아보는 게 좋을 것 같아요.

p.20

Vocabulary & Expression

하도

하도 means ***so, too.*** It is used with -아/어서 when one gives the reason for why a certain status or behavior is at an excessive level. It can be used in both positive and negative situations. It is used for informal occasions in spoken language.

ex A: 유키 씨, 그 공연 전부터 보고 싶다고 했잖아요. 예매했어요?
B: 아니요. 표가 하도 비싸서 못 샀어요.

Script

(1) Staff	Hello, this is Ewha Theater.
Julia	Hello, I found this number on your website. I have an inquiry about the show.
Staff	All right, which show do you want to see?
Julia	I want to see the play "The Dwarf who loved Snow White." But I'm worried it might be too difficult for kids to understand.
Staff	Well, you don't need to worry about that. It's directed in a style that is easy and enjoyable for children. Also, it is not that long so the children won't get bored.
Julia	On the website it says it is suitable even for adults to watch together.
Staff	Yes. Many people who have seen the play say the story is very moving and not childish at all.
Julia	I see. Thank you for your kind explanation.
Staff	My pleasure. Please contact us if you have further inquiries.
(2) Wang Qian	Julian, are you available on Friday evening?
Julian	This coming Friday? Yes, why?
Wang Qian	Do you want to see a show with me? Sarah gave me the tickets.
Julian	Really? What kind of show is it?
Wang Qian	Oh, it's a traditional Korean performance where the actors wear masks. She said that the expressions of the masks were so interesting and amazing that she saw the show three times.
Julian	Really? Is it that good?
Wang Qian	Yeah, she said the play was too good to see alone. She also said that it would be a good chance to learn about Korean culture.
Julian	That's great. I haven't seen any traditional performances yet but have been waiting for the opportunity.
Wang Qian	All right, let's go together then.

Answers

(1) ① The staff member is telling Julia that according to audience reviews, the play is very moving and not childish at all.

(2) ④ Sarah saw this show three times because the expressions of the masks were so interesting and amazing. It was not because she wanted to learn about Korean culture.

Vocabulary & Expression

돈이 하나도 아깝지 않다

돈이 하나도 아깝지 않다 means ***to be worth the money***. This indicates that something is so valuable that it is well worth the money paid for it. 하나도 can be used with –지 않다, –지 못하다, 아니다, or 없다 and means one does not feel a certain way about something at all, or not even a little bit.

ex A: 회사 앞 한식집 가 봤어요? 좀 비싸지만 정말 맛있대요.
B: 네, 저도 가 봤는데 음식이 하도 맛있어서 돈이 하나도 아깝지 않았어요.

ex A: 여행은 잘 다녀왔어요? 사진도 많이 찍었고요?
B: 카메라를 챙겨 갔는데 다음날 고장이 나서 사진을 하나도 못 찍었어요.

ex A: 계속 배고프다고만 하지 말고 뭐라도 좀 먹어.
B: 냉장고에 먹을 게 하나도 없어. 라면이나 먹어야겠다.

ex A: 태권도를 배우려고 하는데 너무 어려울까 봐서 망설여져요.
B: 하나도 안 어려우니까 걱정 마세요. 제가 가르쳐 줄게요.

Dialogue

Kim Sujin	Julian, do you like musicals? I think I heard before that you liked them.
Julian	Yes, I do like them. When I was in France, I went to see musicals on and off, but I haven't got round to seeing them in Korea.
Kim Sujin	Then, do you want to go see a musical this weekend?
Julian	Sure. Is there anything good to see these days?
Kim Sujin	My friend told me that "Finding Kim Jongwuk" was good. She said it was a perfect stress-reliever since it features exciting music and dance.
Julian	Really? What's it about?
Kim Sujin	It's about first love. It features Kim Min-ho, who's hugely popular right now, and my friend said that his acting was really good. She also said that his comic acting was better than she had expected.
Julian	Really? Then, let's go see it together. How much are the tickets?
Kim Sujin	She said it was about 100,000 won. It's a bit expensive, isn't it?
Julian	100,000 won? Wow, that's pretty expensive.
Kim Sujin	I read some online reviews saying that the ticket was expensive but well worth the money. We can get a 20 percent discount if we book online.
Julian	All right. Then, let's hurry up and book tickets online as well.

Grammar Focus

–냬요 is used when one conveys to another person a question that he/she has heard from a third party. –재요 is used when one conveys to another person something the third party has suggested or proposed. These are both indirect speech contractions of –냐고 하다 and –자고 하다 respectively. –(으)래요 is used when one conveys to another person something the third party has requested or ordered, and is a contraction of –(으)라고 하다. –재요 and –(으)래요 are attached to verbs.

Basic form	–냬요	–았/었냬요	–(으)ㄹ 거냬요
바쁘다	바쁘냬요	바빴냬요	–
좋다	좋으냬요	좋았냬요	–
가다	가냬요	갔냬요	갈 거냬요
먹다	먹냬요	먹었냬요	먹을 거냬요
만들다	만드냬요	만들었냬요	만들 거냬요
친구이다	친구냬요	친구였냬요	–
학생이다	학생이냬요	학생이었냬요	–

Basic form	–재요	–(으)래요
하다	하재요	하래요
먹다	먹재요	먹으래요
만들다	만들재요	만들래요

ex A: 형, 찌개 먹어 봐. 엄마가 찌개가 좀 싱겁냬. 싱거우면 소금을 좀 넣으래.
B: 음, 별로 안 싱거운데? 난 소금 안 넣어도 돼.

ex A: 여보세요. 아빠, 엄마가 오늘 몇 시에 퇴근하시냬요.
집들이 준비를 같이 해야 하니까 집에 빨리 들어오시래요.
B: 그래. 5시쯤 도착하겠다고 전해 줘.

ex A: 그 친구한테 연락 왔어? 싸운 후로 연락 없었어?
B: 어제 전화 왔었어. 아직도 자기한테 화가 났냬.
그리고 미안하다고 하면서 이번 주말에 만나서 이야기하재.

ex A: 오늘 회사에서 무슨 일 없었어요? 제가 왜 결근했는지 물어보는 사람 없었어요?
B: 안 그래도 과장님께서 민수 씨 어디가 아프냐고 하셨어요.
내일 다 같이 삼계탕이라도 먹으러 가재요.

ex A: 흐엉 씨한테서 아까 전화 왔었다고요? 흐엉 씨가 뭐래요?
B: 희진 씨 언제 이사할 거냬요. 그리고 이사를 도와줄 사람이 있냬요.
없으면 자기가 도와주겠대요.

ex A: 왕치엔 씨가 아까 나한테 뭐랬어? 내가 과장님하고 이야기하고 있어서 잘 못 들었거든.
B: 오후 4시까지는 회의가 있으니까 그 이후에 연락 달래요.

Grammar Focus

- The indirect speech contractions –냬요, –재요, and –(으)래요 are the same as –ㄴ/는대요 when one and another person have a close relationship with each other. It is not appropriate to use this expression in formal or official occasions.

  ex 이것으로 회의를 마치겠습니다. 회의 후에 팀장님께서 회식을 하자고 하셨습니다. (○)
  이것으로 회의를 마치겠습니다. 회의 후에 팀장님께서 회식을 하재요. (×)

- –지 말재요 is used when conveying the imperative sentence –지 맙시다 to another person.

  ex A: 줄리앙 씨, 여자 친구하고 주말에 놀이공원에 간다면서요?
  B: 그러려고 했는데 여자 친구가 이번 주말에 가지 말재요. 바쁘다고 다음에 가재요.

- –지 말래요 is used when conveying the imperative sentence –지 마세요 to another person.

  ex A: 이번 주 금요일이 아키라 씨 딸 돌잔치인데 무슨 선물을 사 가는 게 좋을까요?
  B: 그런데 아키라 씨가 축하해 주러 오는 것만으로도 고맙다고 하면서 선물은 사 오지 말래요.

- When the verb 주다 is used with the indirect expression –(으)라고 하다, the form changes to 달라고 하다 or 주라고 하다 depending on what the object in the sentence is referring to. When the target of the object is the speaker, 달래요 is used to convey the original words, and when the target is a third person 주래요 is used to convey the original words. The same applies to –아/어 주다.

ex
창호: 마이클 씨, (저에게) 물 좀 주세요. 그리고 유키에게 우유를 갖다 주세요.
⇨
마이클: 창호가 (자기에게) 물 좀 달래요. 그리고 유키에게 우유를 갖다 주래요.

ex
희진: 성호야, 내일 나 좀 도와줘. 그리고 소연에게 이 책도 전해줘.
⇨
성호: 소연아, 희진이 내일 (자기) 좀 도와 달래. 그리고 너한테 이 책도 전해 주래.
소연: 응, 고마워.

Answers

① A: 누구한테서 온 메시지야?
B: 줄리앙한테서 왔는데 오늘 저녁에 자기 집에서 파티하는데 올 거냬. 시험도 끝났으니까 신나게 놀재. 다른 친구들도 많이 데려오래.

② A: 누구한테서 온 메시지예요?
B: 제이슨 씨한테 왔는데 이번 주 토요일에 등산 모임이 있냬요. 자기도 참석하고 싶은데 모이는 장소와 시간 좀 알려 달래요. 그리고 등산 후에 오랜만에 같이 식사하재요.

Grammar Focus

-다니 is used when one shows that he/she is very surprised by or cannot believe the thing that he/she is talking about. -다니 is also used when one is surprised by something that happened in the past. In the following clause, 놀랍다, 대단하다, 믿을 수 없다, 믿어지지 않다, 말도 안 되다, or 어이가 없다 are usually used.

Basic form	-다니	Basic form	-다니
바쁘다	바쁘다니	살다	살다니
좋다	좋다니	친구이다	친구라니
오다	오다니	학생이다	학생이라니

ex A: 마리 씨는 아직 안 왔어요?
B: 네. 다른 사람도 아니고 마리 씨가 약속 시간에 늦다니 정말 이상해요.

ex A: 영민 씨가 10억 원짜리 복권에 당첨됐대요.
B: 뭐라고요? 그렇게 많은 돈을 받게 되다니 믿을 수 없어요.

ex A: 너무 배가 고파서 혼자서 갈비 3인분을 먹었어요.
B: 아무리 배가 고파도 그렇지 그걸 다 먹다니 말도 안 돼요.

ex A: 저기 안나 씨 옆에 있는 여자가 안나 씨 쌍둥이 여동생이래요.
B: 네? 하나도 안 닮았는데 두 사람이 쌍둥이라니 믿어지지 않아요.

Focus Plus

- A sentence may end simply with 다니(요).

ex A: 저기 저 사람 가수 현지 아니에요?
B: 정말이네요! 좋아하던 가수를 바로 눈앞에서 보다니…….

ex A: 제이슨 씨가 이번 학기에도 장학금을 받았대요.
B: 한두 번도 아니고 4년 내내 장학금을 받다니요…….

Answers

① A: 유키 씨가 약속 시간에 1시간이나 늦었대요.
B: 그래요? 항상 약속 시간을 잘 지키는 유키 씨가 1시간이나 늦다니 정말 이상하네요.

② A: 창수 씨가 다음 달에 졸업한대요.
B: 그래요? 창수 씨가 다음 달에 졸업을 하다니 시간이 정말 빨리 가네요.

③ A: 아프리카에 눈이 온대요.
B: 정말요? 아프리카에 눈이 오다니 말도 안 돼요.

④ A: 마사코 씨에게 남자 친구가 생겼대요.
B: 정말요? 마사코 씨에게 남자 친구가 생기다니 정말 부러워요.

⑤ A: 김밥이 한 줄에 10,000원이래요.
B: 뭐라고요? 김밥이 한 줄에 10,000원이라니 어이가 없네요.

 p.26

Vocabulary & Expression

흥행작

흥행작 means ***box office success***. It indicates a play or movie that is successful at the box-office.

ex A: 올해 최고의 영화 흥행작은 뭔가요?
B: 올해 초 개봉되어 1,000만 관객을 넘은 〈어제 그리고 오늘〉이라는 영화가 올해 최고의 흥행작이라고 할 수 있습니다.

Script

Akira	Huong, Frank suggested we should go see a play this weekend if nothing's up.
Huong	It's fine with me. What play are we going to see?
Akira	Well, Frank said he heard "Stickleback Fish" was good, and suggested we go see that.
Huong	"Stickleback Fish?" What's it about?
Akira	It's about love between father and son. It was the biggest box-office hit last year, so there's a special repeat performance. Oh, it also features the movie star Kim Minho.
Huong	Huh? What? The movie star Kim Minho is acting in a play?
Akira	Yes. It was his first play and he received an award for it. He acted as the father and the reviews were really good. They said his acting moved the audience.
Huong	Wow! Amazing! He received an award for his first play!
Akira	Isn't it amazing? His acting must have been really good. The play should be worth seeing. Oh, guess what! I checked the theater website and the actors will be signing autographs after the play.
Huong	Really? All right, let's go see it. You know I like Kim Minho. When are we going?
Akira	Are you okay with Sunday? I only have time on Sunday. I'm busy on Saturday.
Huong	Yeah, that's fine. What about Frank?
Akira	Frank said anytime would be fine with him. He told me to arrange the time with you and let him know.
Huong	Yeah? Ok, then I'll call Frank. Wow. I finally get to see Kim Minho in person.

Answers

(1) ② It is not Frank but Akira who suggested they should go see a play on Sunday.

(2) ④ Akira said that this performance is a special one but he didn't say whether it was the last chance to see the play.

(3) ④ Akira and Huong are talking about the movie star Kim Minho, who performs in the play. Akira is telling Huong that Kim Minho acts as the father in the play and that his performance was so good that he received not only an award but also good reviews.

Vocabulary & Expression

애매하다

애매하다 means ***to be vague***. It means something is not clearly one thing or another. It can be used with a verb in the form -기가 애매하다 to indicate that it is difficult to decide whether to do something or not. It can also be used with a noun in the form N이/가 애매하다.

ex A: 요즘 날씨가 아침에는 쌀쌀하고 낮에는 너무 더워요.
B: 맞아요. 일교차가 이렇게 클 때에는 옷 입기가 정말 애매해요.

요기하다

요기하다 means ***to ease one's hunger***. This indicates that one eats just enough to take the edge off one's hunger rather than having a substantial meal. Similar expressions are 간단하게 먹다, 대충 때우다 and so on. 때우다 means that one substitutes a meal with something light.

ex A: 점심시간이 한참 지났네요. 하오밍 씨는 배 안 고파요?
B: 저도 배고파요. 근데 지금은 그냥 요기만 하고 이따가 저녁을 제대로 먹는 게 어때요?

Dialogue

Akira	Hello.
Jason	Hi, it's me. Ewha Band is performing and Yuki suggested we should go see it together. You're coming, right?
Akira	Ewha Band? I can't miss a performance by Ewha Band. When is it?
Jason	It is at 5:00 p.m. next Saturday and Sunday. Yuki asked which you prefer.
Akira	Saturday would be good since we have to go to class the day after Sunday. What about the tickets?
Jason	Yuki said she would book if I let her know what day we prefer. I'll ask Yuki to book a ticket for you too.
Akira	All right, thanks. Wow, I can't believe that I'll finally hear Ewha Band playing live. It's like a dream to me.
Jason	I knew you'd like it.
Akira	Yeah? But dinner time is a bit vague since the concert is at 5:00 p.m. What are you going to do about dinner?
Jason	Well, I was going to have a quick bite before the concert.
Akira	I heard there's a famous restaurant with great food near the concert hall. Why don't we try it out after the concert? Let's have a nice meal and a good talk since we haven't done that for a long time.
Jason	It's fine with me. I'll tell Yuki, too.

Vocabulary & Expression

진출하다

진출하다 means ***to advance into, to enter.*** This indicates to move forward by widening one's range of activities or power. It can be used in expressions such as 무대에 진출하다, 결승전에 진출하다, or 해외 시장에 진출하다.

ex 한국 축구팀이 드디어 결승전에 진출하게 되었다.

ex 영화배우 류지현이 일본에 진출해서 큰 인기를 얻고 있다.

발걸음을 집으로 향하다

발걸음을 집으로 향하다 means ***to head towards home.*** It indicates to go back home. 발걸음을 N(으)로 향하다 means to head toward a certain direction or place. It is generally used in written language such as novels, travel essays, or reviews.

ex 우리는 서울에 있는 고궁을 모두 구경한 후 서울의 야경을 보기 위해 발걸음을 남산으로 향했다.

입을 다물 수가 없다

입을 다물 수가 없다 means ***to be open-mouthed with surprise.*** It indicates such a state of astonishment upon seeing or hearing something that one cannot close one's mouth. It is used to emphasize great surprise or amazement.

ex A: 마리 씨는 정말 대단한 것 같아요. 말하기 대회에서 대상을 받다니.
B: 마리 씨가 정말요? 1년 전에는 한국어를 한마디도 못 했었는데 놀라워서 입을 다물 수가 없네요.

Reading Guide

This passage is about a person's feelings and thoughts after watching a performance. Read it thinking about how a report is written in terms of contents and organization.
(☞『이화 한국어 3-2』 p.30)

Answers

(1) ④ This is a review of a concert. It is a piece of writing about one's feelings and thoughts after watching a performance.

(2) ④ In the first paragraph, "Nanta" is introduced as a play without dialogue, composed only of the rhythms of samulnori, Korean traditional percussion quartet. It is not a play performed in Korean. Moreover, it is appropriate for foreigners, since there is no dialogue.

p.33

Vocabulary Expansion

–거리다 is attached to the words for movement or sound to indicate that the movement or sound is continual or very severe.

허우적거리다
to flounder, to flail about

This means to shake one's feet and hands back and forth repeatedly.
ex 영민 씨가 바다에 빠져 허우적거리는 수진 씨를 구했다.

꼬르륵거리다
(stomach) to rumble

This expresses the sound from one's stomach when one is hungry.
ex 배가 너무 고파서 1시간째 배가 계속 꼬르륵거린다.

두근거리다
(heart) to pound, to palpitate

This expresses the sound of one's heart beating in excitement or worry.
ex 매일 똑같은 일상에서 벗어나 아무도 나를 모르는 곳으로 여행을 떠난다는 것은 가슴이 두근거리는 일이다.

두리번거리다
to look around

This expresses the appearance of someone repeatedly looking around with eyes wide open.
ex 주위를 아무리 두리번거려도 내가 아는 사람은 보이지 않는다.

반짝거리다
to glitter, to sparkle

This means that a small piece of light keeps shining on and off.
ex 저기 저 별은 다른 별들보다 유난히 반짝거리는 것 같다.

중얼거리다
to mutter

This means one keeps talking to oneself in a low voice that others cannot hear.
ex 나는 영어 단어를 외울 때 혼자서 중얼거리면서 외워야 잘 외워진다.

투덜거리다
to grumble

This means to keep complaining about something in a low voice that others can barely hear.
ex 민호 씨가 매사에 불만이 많고 투덜거려서 그런지 민호 씨를 좋아하는 사람이 별로 없다.

깔깔거리다
to laugh out loud, to burst out laughing

This means that one can't hold back one's laughter and keeps laughing out loud.
ex A: 주말에 본 연극이 그렇게 재미있었다면서요?
B: 네. 하도 재미있어서 연극을 보는 내내 배꼽을 잡고 깔깔거렸어요.

Vocabulary Check

Part 1 준비합시다 01

- 모집하다 — to recruit
- 공연이 열리다 — (performance) to be held
- 할인 혜택 — discount
- 연예 — entertainment
- 결혼식을 올리다 — to hold a wedding ceremony
- 예정 — schedule
- 올림픽 — the Olympics
- 금메달을 따다 — to win a gold medal
- 목에 걸다 — to hang something around one's neck
- 감격 — deep emotion

Part 1 준비합시다 02

- 판 — board
- 아깝다 — to be worthy of

Part 1 들어 봅시다

- 유치하다 — to be childish, to be immature
- 연출되다 — to be directed
- 적당하다 — to be appropriate
- 탈 — mask

Part 1 말해 봅시다

- 딱 — just, perfectly
- 제격이다 — to be perfect
- 안성맞춤 — to be just the thing (for)
- 제값 — proper price, fair price
- 한창 — at the full
- 주방 — kitchen
- 벌어지다 — to take place, to occur
- 단체 — group

Part 2 준비합시다 01

- 참석하다 — to attend

Part 2 준비합시다 02

- 주인공 — protagonist, hero
- 역할 — role
- 복권 — lottery
- 당첨되다 — to win
- 어이가 없다 — to be surprised, to be shocked

Part 2 들어 봅시다

- 흥행하다 — to be a hit, to be a success
- 그리다 — to draw
- 특별 공연 — special performance
- 상을 받다 — to win an award
- 뛰어나다 — to excel (in)
- 원래 — originally
- 출연하다 — to appear, to act (in a play, movie etc.)
- 평을 받다 — to receive a review

Part 2 말해 봅시다

- 여부 — whether~
- 상상하다 — to imagine
- 반드시 — certainly, surely
- 요기하다 — to ease one's hunger
- 때우다 — to eat something light
- 애매하다 — to be vague
- 소문나다 — to become well-known

Part 3 읽어 봅시다

- 대사 — lines, dialogue
- 사물놀이 — samulnori (Korean traditional percussion quartet)
- 진출하다 — to advance, to enter
- 깜짝 결혼식 — surprise wedding ceremony
- 경쾌하다 — to be cheerful
- 주방장 — chef

- 맞추다 to adjust, to match
- 재미를 더하다 to add to the fun
- 물을 튀기다 to splash water
- 북을 두드리다 to beat a drum
- 인상적 impressive
- 입을 다물다 to close one's mouth
- 자체 itself
- 가득하다 to be full
- 발걸음 footsteps
- 가슴이 뛰다 the heart beats
- 소재 material

Part 3 어휘를 늘려 봅시다

- 툭하면 easily, often
- 삶 life

Topic Vocabulary

Performance

- 관객의 마음을 사로잡다 to capture the hearts of the audience
- 문화생활을 하다 to enjoy culture
- 공연을 시작하다 to start a performance
- 공연을 마치다 to end a performance
- 공연을 준비하다 to prepare a performance
- 영화가 개봉하다 a movie is released
- 막을 내리다 to lower the curtain
- 막을 올리다 to raise the curtain
- 무대를 꾸미다 to decorate the stage
- 무대에 오르다 to put on the stage
- 공연이 끝나다 to have a performance end
- 입장권을 사다 to buy a ticket
- 감독 director
- 출연자가 결정되다 to have the cast decided
- 표를 예매하다 to book a ticket

PART1 준비합시다 01 • –아/어지다

p.38

Grammar Focus

–아/어지다 means that the subject of a sentence comes to do something or be in a certain condition through external influence. It is attached to a verb and turns the object in an active sentence into the subject of a passive sentence. In the case of verbs ending with –뜨리다, –지다 is attached to the verb and –뜨리다 is omitted.

Basic form	–아/어지다	Basic form	–아/어지다
정하다	정해지다	찢다	찢어지다
지우다	지워지다	짓다	지어지다
끄다	꺼지다	부수다	부서지다
켜다	켜지다	누르다	눌러지다
Basic form	**–지다**	**Basic form**	**–지다**
빠뜨리다	빠지다	쓰러뜨리다	쓰러지다
떨어뜨리다	떨어지다	무너뜨리다	무너지다
넘어뜨리다	넘어지다	망가뜨리다	망가지다

ex A: 한글은 언제 만들어졌어요?
B: 한글은 1443년에 만들어졌어요.

ex A: 안나 씨 송별회 날짜는 정해졌어요?
B: 아니요, 아직 정해지지 않았어요. 날짜가 정해지면 다시 연락할게요.

ex A: 민호와 연락이 되니?
B: 아니. 졸업 후에 나도 민호와 연락이 끊어졌어. 나도 민호 소식이 너무 궁금하네.

ex A: 다 고쳤습니다. 전원 버튼을 한번 눌러 보세요. 화면에 불이 들어오면 전원이 켜진 겁니다.
B: 네. 버튼도 잘 눌러지고 전원도 켜지네요.

ex A: 지난여름에 한국에 비가 그렇게 많이 왔다면서요?
B: 네. 비가 많이 와서 피해가 컸다고 들었어요.
나무가 부러지거나 쓰러졌고 집이 무너진 곳도 있대요.

ex A: 휴대 전화가 고장 난 모양이에요. 통화 소리가 잘 안 들려요.
B: 어제 떨어뜨렸다고 했지요? 그때 망가진 것 같으니까 얼른 고치러 가 보세요.

ex A: 이 기계의 장점이 뭔지 좀 설명해 주시겠습니까?
B: 10분 동안 사용하지 않으면 자동으로 전원이 꺼집니다. 전기를 절약하는 데에 큰 도움이 되지요.

ex A: 이 펜은 꽤 비싸군요. 특별한 이유가 있나요?
B: 이 펜은 유리나 비닐에도 써지고 쉽게 지워지지도 않아서 다른 펜들보다 가격이 조금 비쌉니다.

Focus Plus

- When changing an active sentence into a passive sentence using –아/어지다, the object of the active sentence becomes the subject of the passive sentence. Then, 이/가 or 은/는 are attached to the changed subject of the passive sentence. The subject of the active sentence is used with 에 의해 and is placed in front of the verb. In this case, N에 의해 is usually omitted, unless it is the information the speaker wants to emphasize.

ex

Active sentence	N1이/가	N2을/를		V
	세종대왕이	한글을	언제	만들었어요?
	×	↓		↓
Passive sentence	N1에 의해	N2이/가		V+아/어지다
	(세종대왕에 의해)	한글이	언제	만들어졌어요?

ex

Active sentence	N1이/가	N2을/를		V
	사람들이	약속을	내일로	미뤘어요.
	×	↓		↓
Passive sentence	N1에 의해	N2이/가		V+아/어지다
	(사람들에 의해)	약속이	내일로	미뤄졌어요.

- When –아/어지다 is used with an adjective (See 『이화 한국어 2–2』 Chapter 15, p.152), it means that something gradually reaches a certain condition.

ex A: 이번 주말에 비가 많이 온대요.
B: 그래요? 비가 오고 나면 앞으로 날씨가 더 추워지겠네요.

ex A: 어제 마이클 씨를 우연히 만났는데 전보다 얼굴이 많이 좋아졌던데요.
B: 저도 그렇게 느꼈어요. 처음 한국에 왔을 때는 힘들어 했는데 한국 생활에 점점 익숙해지고 있는 것 같아요.

Answers

작년 여름에 비가 많이 오던 날 저는 부엌에서 저녁 식사를 준비하고 있었습니다. 그런데 갑자기 지진이 났습니다. 접시들이 싱크대에서 떨어지면서 바닥에서 깨졌습니다. 그리고 물병 안에 있던 물도 쏟아졌습니다. 장식장은 쓰러지면서 부서졌습니다. 지진이 멈춘 후에도 며칠 동안 전기가 들어오지 않아서 전등이 켜지지 않았습니다. 그날 지진은 평생 잊을 수 없을 겁니다.

Grammar Focus

–아/어야지요 is used when the speaker wants to say that the listener or someone else should have done something but did not do it, or that a certain condition or situation should have turned out to be a certain way but did not. The negative form is –지 말아야지요.

Basic form	–아/어야지요	–았/었어야지요
크다	커야지요	컸어야지요
작다	작아야지요	작았어야지요
쉽다	쉬워야지요	쉬웠어야지요
쉬다	쉬어야지요	쉬었어야지요
쓰다	써야지요	썼어야지요
아끼다	아껴야지요	아꼈어야지요
듣다	들어야지요	들었어야지요
만들다	만들어야지요	만들었어야지요

ex A: 이 제품은 품질이 좋은데 왜 고객들에게 인기가 없을까요?
B: 가격이 비싸잖아요. 물건이 잘 팔리려면 질도 좋고 가격도 저렴해야지요.

ex A: 여보, 이 정도 크기의 집이면 우리 식구가 살기에 충분하지 않을까요?
B: 이것보단 좀 더 넓어야지요. 애들도 곧 학교에 들어가잖아요.

ex A: 내년에 유학을 가려고 하는데 뭐부터 알아봐야 할까요?
B: 그럼 제일 먼저 유키 씨가 다닐 학교와 살 집부터 알아봐야지요.

ex A: 여보, 건강을 생각해서 올해에는 담배를 꼭 끊어야지요.
B: 알겠어요. 이번에는 반드시 끊을게요.

ex A: 시험 접수 기간이 다음 주까지인 줄 알았는데 어제 끝나서 신청을 못 했어요.
B: 그렇게 중요한 건 잘 확인했어야지요.

ex A: 이번 휴가 때 여행을 가려고 계획을 세웠었는데 돈이 없어서 못 갈 것 같아요.
B: 여행을 가려고 했으면 먼저 돈부터 모았어야지요.

Answers

① A: 입맛이 없어서 저녁 식사를 안 했어요.
B: 건강을 위해서 조금이라도 먹었어야지요.

② A: 시험 준비를 못 해서 시험을 못 봤어요.
B: 시험공부는 평소에 미리미리 했어야지요.

③ A: 이번 달 전기세가 너무 많이 나왔어요.
B: 전기를 아껴 썼어야지요.

④ A: 옷을 얇게 입어서 감기에 걸렸어요.
B: 옷을 따뜻하게 입고 다녔어야지요.

⑤ A: 오늘 낼 숙제를 집에 놓고 왔어요.
B: 숙제를 잘 챙겼어야지요.

Vocabulary & Expression

실수로

실수로 means ***by mistake***. It indicates one has done something without intending do it, or by accident.

ex A: 실수로 삭제 버튼을 눌러서 사진이 다 지워졌어요.
B: 서비스 센터에 가서 이야기해 보세요. 지워진 사진들을 복구할 수 있을 거예요.

Script

(1) Lee Sujeong	Jason, you know you're in charge of taking pictures at the picnic tomorrow, right? Don't forget to bring your camera.
Jason	Oh, I should have told you before. My camera is broken so I have to use someone else's.
Lee Sujeong	Is your camera broken?
Jason	Yes. I accidentally dropped it on the floor and the lens is broken.
Lee Sujeong	Ouch. You should've been more careful.
Jason	I know.
Lee Sujeong	But you can use it again after you change the lens.
(2) Yuki	Oh, no! I spilled water on my laptop.
Haoming	Wipe it up quickly! Here, use these napkins.
Yuki	Thanks. I hope nothing's wrong...
Haoming	How is it? Is your laptop working?
Yuki	Huh? The keyboard doesn't work. There seems to be something wrong with it.
Haoming	Then turn off the power quickly. When your laptop gets wet, you should turn off the power first.
Yuki	Really? All right. It's brand-new. What should I do?
Haoming	Hurry up and go get it fixed. It'll be all right.
(3) Wang Xian	Akira, you always listen to music on the subway. How come you're not listening to music today?
Akira	My mp3 is broken.
Wang Xian	Didn't you say it was broken before?
Akira	Yeah. It suddenly turned off while I was listening to music last time. But I can't even turn the power on this time.
Wang Xian	What happened to it?
Akira	I forgot to take the mp3 out of my pocket before I put my pants in the washing machine.
Wang Xian	Whew, you should have checked your pockets first.

Answers

(1) ② The woman said the camera should work if the lens is replaced, and the man has not replaced the lens yet.

(2) ③ The woman spilled water on her new laptop, so the keyboard is not working. The woman said the laptop seemed to be broken.

(3) ② The mp3 is not working because the pants were mistakenly put in the washing machine with the mp3 still in the pocket. But the man did not say he would buy a new mp3.

Vocabulary & Expression

배터리를 빼다

배터리를 빼다 means ***to take out the battery.*** This indicates separating the battery from a cellular phone and taking it out. 배터리를 갈다 means to replace a worn-out battery with a new one. 배터리를 충전하다 means to recharge a battery. 배터리가 없다, 배터리가 나가다, and 배터리가 떨어지다 means the battery has run out.

ex A: 어서 오세요. 어떻게 오셨어요?
B: 휴대 전화 배터리가 고장 나서 사러 왔는데요.
A: 네. 배터리를 빼서 주시겠어요? 손님 휴대 전화에 맞는 배터리를 찾아 드리겠습니다.

ex A: 지금 휴대 전화 배터리가 거의 없어서 전화가 끊어질 것 같아. 배터리 갈고 다시 전화할게.
B: 응, 알겠어.

ex A: 여보, 오늘 하루 종일 휴대 전화가 꺼져 있던데 무슨 일 있었어요?
B: 별일은 없었어요. 그런데 너무 바빠서 휴대 전화 배터리를 충전할 시간도 없었어요.

Dialogue

Julian: Sora, I'm sorry but can we have lunch some other time?
Lee Sora: Why? Did something happen?
Julian: Yeah, my cell phone's broken so I have to go to the service center. The only time I can go is at lunch time.
Lee Sora: Really? That's why you didn't answer the phone yesterday when I called. Anyway, which part is broken?
Julian: It won't turn on when I press the power button. It's so irritating to be without a phone.
Lee Sora: I know. But what happened to it?
Julian: I accidentally dropped it in the sink while I was washing my hands yesterday. There's been something wrong with it since then.
Lee Sora: You dropped the phone in the sink? So what did you do?
Julian: I turned the power off as soon as I took it out of the water. I was worried that it might be out of order.
Lee Sora: If you dropped your phone in water, you should have taken out the battery first and let it dry.
Julian: Really? I didn't know that. I just turned off the power. It hasn't been long since I bought it. What should I do if it's broken?
Lee Sora: I'm sure it can be fixed. We can have lunch next time. Make sure to go to the service center today.

Grammar Focus

–나 보다 is used when one guesses upon a certain fact or situation. It is attached to verbs, 있다 or 없다, while –(으)ㄴ가 보다 is attached to an adjective. –았/었나 보다 is used to guess a situation from the past and –(으)ㄹ 건가 보다 is used to guess a future situation.

Basic form	–(으)ㄴ가 보다	–았/었나 보다	
아프다	아픈가 보다	아팠나 보다	
작다	작은가 보다	작았나 보다	

Basic form	–나 보다	–았/었나 보다	–(으)ㄹ 건가 보다
자다	자나 보다	잤나 보다	잘 건가 보다
먹다	먹나 보다	먹었나 보다	먹을 건가 보다
살다	사나 보다	살았나 보다	살 건가 보다
재미있다	재미있나 보다	재미있었나 보다	–

Basic form	인가 보다	였/이었나 보다
의사이다	의사인가 보다	의사였나 보다
학생이다	학생인가 보다	학생이었나 보다

ex A: 여보, 민수가 몇 시간째 방에서 안 나오는데 자는 거 아니에요?
B: 공부하나 보지요. 방해가 될 수도 있으니까 방에 들어가지 마세요.

ex A: 마리 씨, 오늘도 빵 먹어요? 요즘 아침밥을 잘 못 챙겨 먹나 봐요.
B: 네. 아침에는 너무 바빠서 밥을 챙겨 먹기가 쉽지 않네요.

ex A: 저기 좀 보세요. 극장 앞에 사람이 정말 많네요.
B: 그러게 말이에요. 저 영화가 어제 개봉했다고 하는데 재미있나 봐요.

ex A: 줄리앙 씨, 소라 씨 얼굴이 안 좋아 보여요. 어디가 아프대요?
B: 아까 머리가 아프다고 했었는데 두통이 좀 심한가 봐요. 정말 안색이 많이 안 좋네요.

ex A: 프랑크 씨, 방금 문 두드리는 소리 못 들었어요?
B: 그래요? 어제 인터넷으로 책을 하나 주문했는데 택배가 왔나 봐요.

ex A: 조쉬 씨가 요즘 안 보이네요. 전화도 안 받고요.
B: 겨울 방학이 시작돼서 고향에 돌아갔나 봐요.

ex A: 마이클 씨가 오늘 정말 멋있게 입고 왔네요. 무슨 일이 있대요?
B: 이번 주에 3년 동안 사귄 여자 친구에게 청혼을 할 거라고 했는데 오늘이 그날인가 봐요.

ex A: 배우 유승우 씨 소식 들었어요? 요즘 노래와 춤 연습을 정말 열심히 하고 있대요.
B: 저도 그 소식 들었어요. 가수로 데뷔할 건가 봐요.

Focus Plus

- 보다 in the expression –나 보다 cannot be used in the past tense form 봤다 or the future tense 볼 것이다. It is always used in the present tense.

  ex 수영 씨가 어제 일찍 퇴근했나 봐요. (○)
  수영 씨가 어제 일찍 퇴근했나 봤어요. (×)
  수영 씨가 어제 일찍 퇴근했나 볼 거예요. (×)

- –나 보다 and –(으)ㄴ/는/(으)ㄹ 것 같다 (See 『이화 한국어 2-1』 Chapter 7, p.129) are both used to guess something, but –나 보다 is used when one guesses based on surrounding circumstances. It cannot be used when one talks about something he/she knows through first-hand experience, but only when guessing based on indirect experience or other grounds. On the other hand, –(으)ㄴ/는 것 같다 is used when one talks about his/her feelings or thoughts on facts he/she has experienced first-hand. –(으)ㄹ 것 같다 is used when one talks about vague guesses, feelings, or thoughts.

  ex 창호 씨는 농구를 잘하나 봐요.
  → The speaker guesses that Changho plays basketball well after hearing about his performance on the court or that he has received an award in a basketball tournament. He has not seen Changho playing basketball with his own eyes.

  ex 창호 씨는 농구를 잘하는 것 같아요.
  → The speaker expresses his/her thoughts after seeing Changho play basketball firsthand.

  ex 창호 씨는 농구를 잘할 것 같아요.
  → The speaker is expressing his/her vague thoughts based on the fact that Changho is tall or good at other sports.

Answers

① A: 마리 씨 좀 보세요. 못 보던 예쁜 정장을 입었네요.
B: 그러게요. 새 정장을 한 벌 장만했나 봐요.

② A: 왕치엔 씨 좀 보세요. 한국어 억양이 정말 자연스럽네요.
B: 그러게요. 한국에서 오래 살았나 봐요.

③ A: 유키 씨 좀 보세요. 하루 종일 싱글벙글 웃고 다니네요.
B: 그러게 말이에요. 기분 좋은 일이 있나 봐요.

④ A: 안나 씨 좀 보세요. 한식 조리사 자격증을 가지고 있네요.
B: 그러게요. 한국 음식에 특별히 관심이 많은가 봐요.

⑤ A: 율리아 씨 좀 보세요. 수업 시간에 꾸벅꾸벅 졸고 있네요.
B: 그러게 말이에요. 어젯밤에 잠을 설쳤나 봐요.

 p.45

Grammar Focus

리 in the phrase -(으)ㄹ 리가 없다 indicates "the reason." -(으)ㄹ 리가 없다 is used when the speaker thinks that the content of the preceding clause is definitely not true or there is no reason or possibility of being so. If the content of the preceding clause happened in the past, -았/었을 리가 없다 is used.

Basic form	-(으)ㄹ 리가 없다	-았/었을 리가 없다
비싸다	비쌀 리가 없다	비쌌을 리가 없다
그렇다	그럴 리가 없다	그랬을 리가 없다
가다	갈 리가 없다	갔을 리가 없다
듣다	들을 리가 없다	들었을 리가 없다
의사이다	의사일 리가 없다	의사였을 리가 없다
학생이다	학생일 리가 없다	학생이었을 리가 없다

ex A: 마이클 씨, 다음 주 회식이 취소됐다면서요?
B: 그럴 리가 없어요. 아까도 팀장님이 저한테 다음 주 회식 장소를 추천해 보라고 하셨는데요.

ex A: 유키 씨가 회사를 그만두고 다음 달에 한국으로 유학을 간대요.
B: 유학을 갈 리가 없어요. 승진해서 기쁘다고 어제 저에게 자랑했거든요.

ex A: 안나 씨는 결혼했나 봐요. 손에 반지를 끼고 있어요.
B: 아닐 거예요. 안나 씨는 남자 친구도 없다고 했는데 결혼을 했을 리가 없어요.

ex A: 혹시 내 지갑 못 봤어?
B: 아니, 못 봤는데. 혹시 집에 놓고 나온 거 아니야?
A: 놓고 왔을 리가 없어. 널 만나러 오는 길에도 지갑에서 돈을 꺼냈거든.

ex A: 유키 씨 오빠는 대학원생인가 봐요.
B: 아니에요. 대학원생일 리가 없어요. 유키 씨가 자기 오빠는 작년에 대학교를 졸업하자마자 취직했다고 했어요.

Answers

① A: 연체료가 있는데요.
B: 그래요? 연체료가 있을 리가 없을 텐데요.
어제 연체료를 냈거든요.다시 한번 확인해 보세요.

② A: 손님, 교통 카드에 잔액이 없는데요.
B: 그래요? 잔액이 없을 리가 없을 텐데요.
아까 잔액을 확인했거든요.
다시 한번 확인해 보세요.

③ A: 맛있게 드셨어요? 식사비는 3만 원입니다.
B: 그래요? 3만 원이 나왔을 리가 없을 텐데요.
비빔밥 하나밖에 안 먹었거든요.
다시 한번 확인해 보세요.

④ A: 동아리 회비가 밀렸네. 내일까지 낼 수 있니?
B: 그래요? 회비가 밀렸을 리가 없을 텐데요.
지난주에 회비를 냈거든요.
다시 한번 확인해 보세요.

⑤ A: 이번 달 하숙비가 안 들어왔는데요.
B: 그래요? 하숙비가 안 들어갔을 리가 없을 텐데요.
어제 입금했거든요. 다시 한번 확인해 보세요.

Vocabulary & Expression

일단

일단 means ***first, initially***. It indicates "to start with" or "before anything else."

ex A: 영민 씨, 라면 끓이는 방법 좀 알려 주세요.
B: 일단 물을 끓이세요. 그리고 물이 끓으면 스프를 넣으세요.

ex A: 가고 싶은 곳 있어요? 어디를 먼저 갈까요?
B: 배고프니까 일단 밥부터 먹고 구경하는 게 어때요?

Script

Wang Xian	Jason, I lost the shoes that I bought yesterday.
Jason	Where did you lose them?
Wang Xian	On the subway. I left the shopping bag on the subway.
Jason	Then have you called the subway station where you left the shopping bag?
Wang Xian	No.
Jason	If you call the station, the staff can look for your lost item. Why didn't you call the station?
Wang Xian	Really? Then I should call the station. But would my shoes still be there?
Jason	No, it's not likely that they're still there. They would have been sent to the lost and found office by now. Why don't you call the lost and found?
Wang Xian	The lost and found?
Jason	Yes. Lost items on the subway are kept in the lost and found office. I went there once to find my briefcase, and there were so many lost items.
Wang Xian	Really? So many people must leave their belongings on the subway, just like me. So, what should I say when I call the lost and found?
Jason	Tell them what you left behind, when and at which station. Tell them what it looks like in detail. Oh, you can also search for lost items on the Internet. Check out the subway's lost and found homepage. You'll be able to see photos of the lost items.
Wang Xian	I see. Thanks for all the information. I'll call the lost and found first.

Answers

(1) ② **When one has left something on the subway, he/she can call the subway station where it was lost so that the station staff can look for it.**

(2) ④ **When an item left on the subway is not claimed by the owner at the station concerned, it is sent to the lost and found. Photos of lost items can be viewed on the homepage of the lost and found.**

(3) ④ **When looking for a lost item at the lost and found, one should explain when and where the item was left behind and what it looks like.**

Vocabulary & Expression

책을 몇 권 사다

책을 몇 권 사다 means ***to buy a few books***. It is not a question as to how many books one has bought, but means that one has bought a small number of books. 몇 is used to ask an unknown number in a question, but it can also be used to express a rather small number. When asking the date, 몇 일 is not used but 며칠 as one word.

ex A: 흐엉 씨, 어디에 가요?
B: 서점에 가는 길이에요. 잡지랑 책을 몇 권 사려고요.

ex A: 여보, 이제 퇴근하려고 하는데 필요한 것 있으면 얘기해요. 슈퍼에서 사 갈게요.
B: 고마워요. 아이들이 좋아하는 과자 몇 개만 사 오세요.

ex A: 이번 휴가에 특별한 계획이 있어요?
B: 친한 친구 결혼식이 있어서 고향에 며칠 다녀올 생각이에요.

Dialogue

Yuki	Oh, no! My wallet is gone! Haoming, I think I lost my wallet.
Haoming	Look again. It must be somewhere.
Yuki	I looked everywhere but I can't find it. It can't be gone. It's strange. I had it when I got on the subway.
Haoming	Did you drop by anywhere before school?
Yuki	I dropped by the bookstore and bought a few books before I came to school.
Haoming	Did you have the wallet in the bookstore?
Yuki	Yes, I did. I paid for the books with the credit card in the wallet. I got the receipt and put it in the wallet...
Haoming	Then did you go anywhere else other than the bookstore? Think carefully.
Yuki	No, I didn't go anywhere else. I came to school straight from the bookstore. I might have left the wallet on the counter after I paid for the books.
Haoming	Then call the bookstore and ask if they have your wallet.
Yuki	Yes. There are so many important things in the wallet. What should I do if I can't find it?
Haoming	You'll find it. If your wallet is not in the bookstore, call the credit card company immediately to suspend your credit card.
Yuki	All right. Thank you, Haoming.

Vocabulary & Expression

제값

제값 means the ***right/proper price***. Related expressions are 제값(을) 하다, 제값(을) 주다, 제값(을) 받다 and so on. 제값(을) 하다 means that something is worth the price. 제값(을) 주다 means one buys something at its original price, without receiving a discount or at a bargain. Likewise, 제값(을) 받다 means one does not sell something cheaply or at a discount but at a proper price.

ex A: 무슨 신발이 이렇게 비싸요?
B: 아주 좋은 재질로 만든 신발이래요. 비싼 만큼 제값을 하겠지요.

ex A: 이 가방 어때요? 어제 쇼핑하다가 싸서 샀는데 지금 보니까 질이 별로 안 좋은 것 같아요.
B: 저도 물건을 살 때 제값을 주고 사지 않으면 품질이 의심스러워서 잘 안 사게 돼요.

다음부터는 이런 일이 없기를 바라다

다음부터는 이런 일이 없기를 바라다 means ***to hope something like this will never happen again***. This expression is used to tell someone who has made a mistake or done something wrong that the speaker hopes the same thing will not happen again. Similar expressions are 두 번 다시 이런 실수가 없기를 바라다 and 앞으로는 이런 일이 일어나지 않기를 바라다.

ex A: 부장님, 죄송합니다. 앞으로는 더욱 꼼꼼히 확인하겠습니다.
B: 그래요, 김 대리. 다음부터는 이런 일이 없기를 바랍니다.

ex A: 과장님, 죄송합니다. 앞으로 더욱 조심하겠습니다.
B: 알겠습니다. 두 번 다시 이런 실수가 없기를 바랍니다.

Reading guide

This is a request to exchange a product which has been posted on the bulletin board of the online shopping mall. Read it carefully and think about why the writer wants to exchange the product and how he/she explains the condition of the product.
(☞『이화 한국어 3-2』 p.50)

Answers

(1) ② This is written not to request a refund but to inform the company that the product is faulty, to request an exchange, and to get a proper explanation from the company.

(2) ③ When the writer opened the package, the wrapping paper around the product was torn. The writer said he/she had tried to call the online shopping mall to make an inquiry but could not get through. The writer said the microwave was ordered online. The writer also said he/she had bought a number of products at this online shopping mall.

Vocabulary Expansion

-되다 turns a noun into a verb when it is attached right after the noun. It indicates the passive voice.

발명되다
to be invented

ex A: 지금까지 발명된 것들 중에서 사람들의 생활을 가장 편리하게 해 준 발명품이 뭐라고 생각하십니까?
B: 라이트 형제에 의해 발명된 비행기가 역사상 가장 위대한 발명품이라고 생각합니다.

발견되다
to be discovered

ex A: 우와, 이건 공룡의 발자국인가요?
B: 네. 지금 보시는 이 화석이 현재까지 발견된 공룡 발자국 화석 중 가장 큰 화석입니다.

개발되다
to be developed

ex 먼지가 있는 곳을 스스로 찾아서 청소하는 로봇이 개발되었다.

ex 세계 최초로 개발된 백신 덕분에 인류의 평균 수명이 연장되었습니다.

사용되다
to be used

ex A: 요즘 자신을 타인에게 알리는 수단으로 SNS가 많이 사용되는 거 같죠?
B: 네. 그래서 그런지 요즘 페이스북이나 트위터 사용자가 늘었어요.

완공되다
to be completed

ex A: 지금 짓고 있는 축구 경기장이 내년에 완공된대요.
B: 저도 어제 뉴스에서 봤는데 디자인이 멋있던데요? 기대가 되네요.

판매되다
to be sold

ex A: 요즘 제일 잘 팔리는 옷이 이거지요? 저도 하나 주세요.
B: 죄송합니다, 손님. 준비된 상품이 모두 판매되었습니다. 물건이 다시 들어오면 연락을 드리겠습니다.

준비되다
to be prepared

ex A: 여보세요. 이화요리교실이지요? 내일이 수업 첫날인데 뭘 준비해 가야 하나요?
B: 필요한 재료는 모두 준비되어 있으니까 그냥 오시면 됩니다.

변경되다
to be changed

ex A: 우리 대학교 동창 모임이 이번 주 토요일 저녁 맞지요?
B: 제이슨 씨도 몰랐나 보네요. 저도 어제 연락을 받았는데 동창 모임이 다음 주 토요일로 변경됐대요.

Vocabulary Check

Part 1 준비합시다 01

- 찢어지다 to be torn
- 인쇄 printing
- 깨지다 to be broken
- 꺼지다 to be turned off
- 켜지다 to be turned on
- 부서지다 to be broken
- 쏟아지다 to be spilled
- 지진이 나다 to have an earthquake occur
- 싱크대 sink
- 장식장 display cupboard
- 쓰러지다 to fall, to collapse
- 전등 lamp, light
- 멈추다 to stop, to halt

Part 1 준비합시다 02

- 상하다 to hurt, to injure
- 분실하다 to lose
- 정지시키다 to stop, to pause
- 입맛 appetite
- 전기세 electricity bill
- 숙제를 내다 to give homework

Part 1 들어 봅시다

- 다운되다 to be down
- 연결 connection
- 재생 play
- 화면 screen
- 자판 keyboard
- 렌즈 lens
- 교체하다 to replace
- 눌러지다 to be pressed
- 물기 moisture

Part 1 말해 봅시다

- 대처 management, handling
- 미루다 to put off, to postpone
- 삭제 deletion
- 충전시키다 to recharge
- 세면대 sink
- 가전제품 home appliances
- 꽂다 to put
- 무시하다 to ignore, to disregard

Part 2 준비합시다 01

- 연기가 나다 to have smoke appear
- 싱글벙글 to be all smiles
- 조리사 cook
- 정장 suit, full dress
- 장만하다 to get, to buy
- 꾸벅꾸벅 drowsily
- 잠을 설치다 to sleep fitfully
- 억양 intonation

Part 2 준비합시다 02

- 세다 to count
- 연체료 late fee, overdue charge
- 잔액 balance
- 회비 (membership) fee
- 하숙비 room and board, boarding expenses
- 입금하다 to deposit

Part 2 들어 봅시다

- 유실물 센터 lost and found (office)
- 보관하다 to keep
- 열차 train

Part 2 말해 봅시다

- 계산대 counter
- 검색하다 to search
- 필기 notes

Part 3 읽어 봅시다

- 요청 demand, request
- 조회 inquiry, check
- 신제품 new product
- 운반하다 to cart, to transport
- 뜯어보다 to open (and see)
- 포장지 wrapping paper
- 먼지가 묻다 to be dusted
- 흠 flaw, defect
- 반송하다 to send back
- 헌 old, worn-out
- 해명 clarification, explanation
- 답변 response, reply
- 요구 사항 requirements
- 당부 request, entreaty

Part 3 어휘를 늘려 봅시다

- 치료제 medicine
- 공룡 dinosaur
- 발자국 footprint
- 발명품 invention

Topic Vocabulary

Problem Solving

- 대책 measure, step
- 문제점 problem
- 발생하다 to happen, to occur
- 원인 cause
- 처리하다 to deal with
- 해결하다 to resolve
- 현상 phenomenon

PART1 준비합시다 01 • -ㄴ/는다면

p.58

Grammar Focus

-ㄴ/는다면 is used when one supposes a certain situation that is hardly likely. It is often accompanied by 만일 and 만약. -ㄴ/는다면 is attached to a verb, while -다면 is attached to an adjective, 있다, and 없다, and (이)라면 to a noun.

Basic form	-다면	Basic form	-ㄴ/는다면	Basic form	(이)라면
크다	크다면	가다	간다면	의사이다	의사라면
작다	작다면	먹다	먹는다면	학생이다	학생이라면
멋있다	멋있다면	돕다	돕는다면	-	-
재미없다	재미없다면	살다	산다면	-	-

ex A: 만약 로봇이 사람 대신 모든 일을 다 한다면 어떻게 될까요?
B: 글쎄요. 그렇게 된다면 많은 사람들이 게을러져서 일자리를 잃지 않을까요?

ex A: 줄리앙 씨, 내년에 여행을 간다면 어디로 가고 싶어요?
B: 한국이나 일본, 태국처럼 프랑스에서 먼 곳으로 여행을 가 보고 싶어요.

ex A: 좋아하는 사람이 있는데 내 마음을 말할 자신이 없어. 그냥 포기해야 할까?
B: 만일 내가 너라면 지금 그 사람에게 가서 고백할 거야. 용기를 내 봐.

Focus Plus

- Both -ㄴ/는다면 and -(으)면 (See『이화 한국어 1-2』Chapter 12, p.85) can be used to assume the possible situation of the preceding clause or express the conditions of the following clause. -ㄴ/는다면 is used to assume a situation that is hardly likely in reality. On the contrary, -(으)면 can be used not only to assume an unlikely situation but also to talk about a high probability of the following clause or the conditions for the situation in the following clause.

ex 제가 만약 복권에 당첨된다면 전 세계를 여행해 보고 싶어요.
네가 시험에 합격한다면 네가 해 달라는 것은 다 해 줄게.

ex 모두 모이면 회의를 시작합시다.
저는 아이스크림을 먹으면 머리가 아파요.

Answers

① A: 투명인간이 된다면 뭘 하고 싶어요?
B: 만약에 투명인간이 된다면 좋아하는 사람의 집에 가서 그 사람이 어떻게 사는지 보고 싶어요.

② A: 내일 지구가 멸망한다면 뭘 하고 싶어요?
B: 만약 그렇게 된다면 오늘은 가족과 시간을 보낼 거예요.

③ A: 여자로 다시 태어난다면 뭘 하고 싶어요?
B: 만약 그럴 수 있다면 화장도 하고 짧은 치마도 입어 보고 싶어요.

④ A: 하루가 30시간이라면 뭘 하고 싶어요?
B: 만약 하루가 30시간이라면 남은 시간 동안 잠을 더 푹 자고 싶어요.

⑤ A: 세계적으로 유명한 영화배우라면 뭘 하고 싶어요?
B: 만약 제가 세계적으로 유명한 영화배우라면 국제 영화제에 꼭 참석해 보고 싶어요.

Grammar Focus

-(으)ㄹ지도 모르다 is used when the speaker guesses a situation with low possibility in the present or future. **-았/었을지도 모르다** is used for an action or situation in the past. It is often accompanied by **혹시** or **어쩌면**.

Basic form	-(으)ㄹ지도 모르다	-았/었을지도 모르다
크다	클지도 모르다	컸을지도 모르다
작다	작을지도 모르다	작았을지도 모르다
어렵다	어려울지도 모르다	어려웠을지도 모르다
그렇다	그럴지도 모르다	그랬을지도 모르다
자다	잘지도 모르다	잤을지도 모르다
먹다	먹을지도 모르다	먹었을지도 모르다
듣다	들을지도 모르다	들었을지도 모르다
살다	살지도 모르다	살았을지도 모르다
친구이다	친구일지도 모르다	친구였을지도 모르다
선생님이다	선생님일지도 모르다	선생님이었을지도 모르다

ex A: 앞으로 100년 후에는 세상이 어떻게 변할까요?
B: 회사로 출근하는 사람이 아무도 없을지도 몰라요. 집에서 컴퓨터로만 일을 해도 될 테니까요.

ex A: 여보, 오늘도 많이 늦어요?
B: 오늘은 일찍 올 수 있을 거예요. 그래도 갑자기 회의가 생기면 혹시 늦을지도 모르니까 기다리지 말고 먼저 자도록 해요.

ex A: 이제 전원 버튼이 잘 눌러지네요. 고맙습니다.
B: 별말씀을요. 손님, 나중에 혹시 도움이 필요할지도 모르니까 제 연락처를 알려 드릴게요. 제품에 이상이 있으면 연락 주세요.

ex A: 유미 씨가 어제 연락도 없이 왜 안 왔을까요?
B: 어제 많이 아팠을지도 몰라요. 며칠 전부터 몸이 안 좋다고 했거든요. 한번 전화해 봐야겠어요.

ex A: 저녁 시간이 지났으니까 마리도 저녁을 먹었겠지?
B: 아까 오늘 수업이 늦게 끝난다고 하던데. 어쩌면 아직 안 먹었을지도 모르니까 연락해 봐.

ex A: 프랑크 씨는 여자 친구가 있나 봐요. 어제 프랑크 씨가 어떤 여자랑 걸어가는 걸 봤거든요.
B: 그래요? 어쩌면 동생일지도 몰라요. 지난주에 동생이 한국에 왔다고 했거든요.

Focus Plus

- 모르다 in the expression -(으)ㄹ지도 모르다 cannot be used in the past tense form 몰랐다. Because it indicates that one is not sure whether something assumed is true or not, it can only be used in the present tense.

  ex 마크 씨가 어제 숙제를 했다고 했지만 안 했을지도 몰라요. (○)
  마크 씨가 어제 숙제를 했다고 했지만 안 했을지도 몰랐어요. (×)

- Both -(으)ㄹ지도 모르다 and -(으)/는/(으)ㄹ 것 같다(See 『이화 한국어 2-1』 Chapter 7, p.129) are used to guess something. -(으)ㄹ지도 모르다 means that one does not know whether the situation in the previous sentences will happen or not, therefore assuming the possibility of the opposite situation. It is not used when the basis of speculation is clear, so it expresses low confidence in the speculated situation. -(으)/는/(으)ㄹ 것 같다 is used when there is greater confidence in the speculated situation than when using -(으)ㄹ지도 모르다. However, it can be used to talk about vague thoughts or feelings without any basis, and therefore can be used with or without a basis for speculation.

  ex (엄마가 일기예보 날씨를 확인하지 못하고 외출하는 아이에게 하는 말)
  날씨가 추울지도 모르니까 옷 따뜻하게 입고 나가. (○)
  날씨가 추울 것 같으니까 옷 따뜻하게 입고 나가. (○)

  ex (엄마가 일기예보 날씨를 확인하고 나서 외출하는 아이에게 하는 말)
  날씨가 추울 것 같으니까 옷 따뜻하게 입고 나가. (○)
  날씨가 추울지도 모르니까 옷 따뜻하게 입고 나가. (×)

Answers

① 50년 후에는 한국이 통일될지도 몰라요.
그래서 우리도 자유롭게 평양에 갈 수 있을지도 몰라요.

② 50년 후에는 외계인이 지구에서 살지도 몰라요.
그래서 매일 아침 출근길에 외계인을 만나게 될지도 몰라요.

③ 50년 후에는 하늘을 날 수 있는 구두가 발명될지도 몰라요.
그렇게 된다면 비행기를 타는 사람들이 없어질지도 몰라요.

④ 50년 후에는 날씨가 더워져서 겨울이 없어질지도 몰라요.
겨울이 없어진다면 북극곰과 펭귄들이 사라질지도 몰라요.

⑤ 50년 후에는 누구나 쉽게 우주여행을 할 수 있을지도 몰라요.
그래서 수학여행을 행성으로 가게 될지도 몰라요.

Vocabulary & Expression

오늘따라

오늘따라 means ***today of all days***. This indicates coincidentally today, for no particular reason. A similar expression is 그날따라.

ex A: 여보세요. 마리 씨, 아직도 오고 있는 중이에요?
B: 미안해요. 오늘따라 차가 많이 막히네요. 조금만 기다려 주세요.

Script

(1) Wang Xian What do you think life will be like in 100 years?

Akira Well, I think people will be more pushed for time 100 years later. As you know, people these days are much busier than people in the old days. So in 100 years, won't people be much busier than they are now? Maybe, people will eat nutritional supplements instead of rice because there's no time to eat.

Wang Xian I love eating delicious food, but if the world in 100 years is like what you just said, then there would be no fun in living.

(2) Haoming Why is the traffic so jammed today of all days?

Mari I know. I think the traffic congestion is getting worse and worse.

Haoming Phew, whenever I'm stuck in traffic, I wish I could be teleported.

Mari Teleported?

Haoming If science keeps on developing, will teleportation be possible in about 100 years?

Mari It could be possible. If everyone can be teleported in the future, there would be no need for cars, airplanes, or spaceships.

(3) Anna Jason, what are you looking at so intently?

Jason The newspaper. Look at this. I think environmental pollution is really serious. It says ice in the North Pole is melting so the polar bear habitat is disappearing. If our environment keeps on being polluted like this, humans may not be able to live on earth any more.

Anna Really? That's serious. If all the ice in the North Pole melts away, it will make the sea level higher and there won't be enough land for people to live on.

Jason Yes. Then people might have to find another planet other than earth. We should start protecting the environment now, before things get that bad.

Answers

(1) ① **The man said people might take nutritional supplements instead of rice because they don't want to waste time eating.**

(2) ④ **It was speculated that teleportation of people might be possible in about 100 years if science keeps on developing.**

(3) ② **As the ice in the North Pole is melting, the habitat for polar bears is disappearing, but polar bears have not become extinct yet.**

Vocabulary & Expression

아니 글쎄

아니 글쎄 means ***Guess what?*** or ***Can you believe it?***. It is used to express astonishment at or emphasize what one is about to say. 글쎄 can be used by the speaker to emphasize what he/she says. Both expressions are used in spoken language.

ex A: 아니 글쎄, 어제 마트에 갔는데 과일 값이 지난달보다 3배 정도 오른 거 있지?
B: 아무리 장마철이라도 그렇지 정말 많이 올랐네.

ex A: 그 이야기 들었어?
B: 무슨 이야기?
A: 대학교 4년 내내 장학금을 탄 사람이 글쎄 바로 수진이었대.

Dialogue

Yuki	Julian, did you see the newspaper this morning? Guess what? The lottery winner this time received the record high payout!
Julian	The winner must be so happy. What luck. What will the winner do with that money?
Yuki	The winner said he would give all the money to charity.
Julian	Wow! Really? That's incredible.
Yuki	Yes. I don't think I could do the same thing.
Julian	But perhaps he's already a wealthy man.
Yuki	You may be right. But no matter how rich he is, it must be difficult to make such a decision.
Julian	That's right. If I won the lottery, I would travel around the world. What would you like to do if you won the lottery, Yuki?
Yuki	Well, if I won the lottery, I'd give everything to my parents. They worked so hard to bring me up.
Julian	You're such a good daughter, Yuki. I wish we could win the lottery to travel around the world, and be good to our parents.
Yuki	Just imagining it makes me happy. But I heard that some people who won the lottery have become rather unhappy.
Julian	It could be possible. Money can't buy happiness. Anyway, shall we go and buy a lottery ticket today?

01 • -(으)ㄴ/는 편이다

p.64

Grammar Focus

-(으)ㄴ/는 편이다 is used when one wants to say that something generally fits or is close to a certain condition rather than being decisively so. -(으)ㄴ 편이다 is attached to an adjective whose stem ends in a consonant, and -ㄴ 편이다 is attached to an adjective whose stem ends in a vowel. -는 편이다 is attached to a verb no matter if its stem ends in a consonant or a vowel. The past tense form is -(으)ㄴ/는 편이었다.

Basic form	-(으)ㄴ/는 편이다	-(으)ㄴ/는 편이었다
짧다	짧은 편이다	짧은 편이었다
덥다	더운 편이다	더운 편이었다
있다	있는 편이다	있는 편이었다
잘하다	잘하는 편이다	잘하는 편이었다
		잘한 편이었다
먹다	먹는 편이다	먹는 편이었다
		먹은 편이었다
만들다	만드는 편이다	만드는 편이었다
		만든 편이었다

ex A: 저는 성격이 좀 예민한 편인 것 같아요.
여행 가서 환경이 바뀌면 잠도 잘 못 자고 음식도 잘 못 먹거든요.
B: 소라 씨도 그래요? 저도 그런 편이에요.

ex A: 영민 씨는 학교에 갈 때 버스를 타요? 지하철을 타요?
B: 저는 지하철은 길이 막힐 걱정이 없으니까 지하철을 자주 이용하는 편이에요.

ex A: 마이클 씨, 떡볶이 안 매워요? 매운 음식도 잘 드시네요.
B: 고향에 있을 때는 잘 못 먹었는데 한국에 살면서 자주 먹어서 그런지 요즘엔 잘 먹는 편이에요.

ex A: 제이슨, 어제 피자 한 판을 혼자 다 먹었다면서?
B: 그래도 난 적게 먹은 편이었어. 진호가 나보다 훨씬 많이 먹었거든.

Answers

① A: 마리 씨는 성격이 급한 편이에요?
차분한 편이에요?
B: 마리 씨는 성격이 급한 편이에요.

② A: 마리 씨는 현실적인 편이에요?
미래지향적인 편이에요?
B: 마리 씨는 현실적인 편이에요.

③ A: 마리 씨는 상상력이 풍부한 편이에요?
상상력이 부족한 편이에요?
B: 마리 씨는 상상력이 부족한 편이에요.

④ A: 마리 씨는 화를 자주 내는 편이에요?
화를 잘 참는 편이에요?
B: 마리 씨는 화를 잘 참는 편이에요.

⑤ A: 마리 씨는 꿈을 잘 기억하는 편이에요?
잘 기억하지 못하는 편이에요?
B: 마리 씨는 꿈을 잘 기억하지 못하는 편이에요.

Grammar Focus

-았/었더라면 is used when one supposes the opposite situation of something that already happened in the past to show his/her regret or frustration. What is supposed is expressed in the preceding clause and what is guessed in the following clause. -(으)ㄹ지도 모르다, -았/었을 것이다, -았/었을 것 같다, and -(으)ㄹ 텐데(요) are expressions used for guessing the content of the following clause.

Basic form	-았/었더라면	Basic form	-았/었더라면
크다	컸더라면	가다	갔더라면
좋다	좋았더라면	먹다	먹었더라면
길다	길었더라면	살다	살았더라면
쉽다	쉬웠더라면	낫다	나았더라면

ex A: 제이슨 씨는 어렸을 때 꿈이 뭐였어요?
B: 농구 선수요. 제 키가 조금만 더 컸더라면 농구 선수가 됐을지도 몰라요.

ex A: 영민아, 어제 소풍 간다고 하지 않았어? 비가 왔는데 갔어?
B: 아니, 못 갔어. 날씨가 좋았더라면 소풍을 갔을 텐데…….

ex A: 흐엉 씨, 지난 학기에 대학교에 지원했다면서요? 입학시험 결과가 어떻게 됐어요?
B: 떨어졌어요. 좀 더 열심히 공부했더라면 입학시험에 합격할 수 있었을 텐데 후회가 돼요.

ex A: 2년 전에 미국에서 유학했을 때 왜 3개월 만에 그만두고 돌아온 거예요?
B: 미국 생활에 적응을 잘 못해서요. 그런데 그때 포기하지 않았더라면 지금은 영어를 유창하게 할 수 있었을 텐데 좀 아쉽네요.

ex A: 어떡하죠? 영화 표가 매진됐어요.
B: 그러니까 제가 어제 예매하자고 했잖아요. 어제 예매했더라면 영화를 볼 수 있었을 거예요.

Focus Plus

- The structure of sentences using -았/었더라면 to convey a sense of regret or dissatisfaction is as follows:

ex

Past fact	Regrettable or dissatisfactory result
나는 어젯밤에 커피를 마셨다.	그래서 잠을 못 잤다.
↓	↓
Supposing the opposite of a past fact	Making a guess about an assumption
나는 어젯밤에 커피를 마시지 않았더라면	잠을 잘 잤을 것이다.

ex

Past fact	Regrettable or dissatisfactory result
나는 공부를 열심히 하지 않았다.	그래서 시험에 떨어졌다.
↓	↓
Supposing the opposite of a past fact	**Making a guess about an assumption**
나는 공부를 열심히 했더라면	시험에 떨어지지 않았을 것이다.

- Both -았/었더라면 and -ㄴ/는다면(See Chapter 10, p.58) are used to suppose something, but -았/었더라면 is used to suppose the opposite of a past fact. -ㄴ/는다면 is used not to suppose the opposite situation of a past fact but a situation that is not likely to happen.

  ex (늦잠을 자서 기차를 놓친 후에 하는 말)
  늦잠을 자지 않았더라면 기차를 놓치지 않았을 거예요.

  ex 한 달 동안 햄버거만 먹는다면 건강이 나빠질 거예요.

Answers

① A: 프랑크 씨, 왜 깁스를 했어요?
B: 계단에서 발을 헛디뎌서 다리를 다쳤어요. 그래서 깁스를 했어요.
계단에서 발을 헛디디지 않았더라면 다리를 다치지 않았을 거예요.

② A: 제이슨 씨, 왜 병원에 입원했어요?
B: 술을 많이 마셔서 건강이 나빠졌어요. 그래서 병원에 입원했어요.
술을 많이 마시지 않았더라면 건강이 나빠지지 않았을 거예요.

③ A: 유키 씨, 왜 학교에 결석했어요?
B: 아이스크림을 많이 먹어서 배탈이 났어요. 그래서 학교에 못 갔어요.
아이스크림을 많이 먹지 않았더라면 배탈이 나지 않았을 거예요.

④ A: 아키라 씨, 여자 친구가 왜 화를 냈어요?
B: 여자 친구 생일을 깜박해서 선물을 준비하지 못했어요. 그래서 여자 친구가 화를 냈어요.
여자 친구 생일을 깜박하지 않았더라면 선물을 준비했을 거예요.

⑤ A: 안나 씨, 왜 안경을 쓰기 시작했어요?
B: 텔레비전을 가까이에서 봐서 눈이 나빠졌어요. 그래서 안경을 쓰기 시작했어요.
텔레비전을 가까이에서 보지 않았더라면 눈이 나빠지지 않았을 거예요.

Vocabulary & Expression

용 꿈을 꾸다

용 꿈을 꾸다 means ***to see a dragon in a dream***. It indicates that one has seen a dragon in one's dreams. One can talk about one's dreams by mentioning an object or situation by saying N 꿈을 꾸다. A similar expression is 꿈에 N이/가 나오다.

ex 보통 용 꿈을 꾸면 아들을 낳고 과일이나 야채 꿈을 꾸면 딸을 낳는다고 믿는다.

ex 꿈에 돼지가 나오면 부자가 될 거라고 믿어서 복권을 사는 사람들이 많다.

Script

Sujin Julia, I hear you're pregnant. Congratulations! Did you have a conception dream?
Julia A conception dream? What's that?
Sujin It's a dream that foretells the birth of a baby. It sometimes reveals the gender of the baby. Or it can reveal something about the personality and future of the baby to be born.
Julia Really? That's amazing. Which dreams indicate a boy and which dreams a girl?
Sujin If you see a tiger, fish, or dragon in your dream it stands for a boy. And if you see a peach, apricot, or ring it stands for a girl.
Julia Did your mother have a conception dream before she gave a birth to you?
Sujin The conception dream for me was dreamed not by my mother but by my grand-mother.
Julia Can someone else have a conception dream for you?
Sujin Yes. A conception dream is usually dreamed by the pregnant woman, but it can also be dreamed by family members such as her husband, parents, brothers or sisters.
Julia I see. What was your conception dream?
Sujin Mine was a tiger.
Julia A tiger? Didn't you say a tiger stood for a boy?
Sujin Yes. A tiger usually signifies a boy but if it's a white tiger, then it could be a girl. If my grandmother had dreamed of a yellow tiger, then I would have been a boy.
Julia You may be right. I wish I could see a peach in my conception dream.
Sujin A peach? Why?
Julia You said a peach was for a girl, right? I want to have a baby girl as pretty as a peach.

Answers

(1) ④ A conception dream is not a dream after the baby is born but before the birth of a child.

(2) ②, ④, ⑥ A dream featuring a tiger, fish, or dragon means that one will have a baby boy.

(3) ④ Julia wants to see a peach in her dream because she wants to have a pretty baby girl, but she has not dreamed of a peach yet.

Vocabulary & Expression

매력에 빠지다

매력에 빠지다 means ***to be infatuated, to be captivated by someone's charm***. It indicates that one is deeply attracted to something or someone. Similar expressions are 매력에 푹 빠지다, 매력에 흠뻑 빠지다, and so on.

ex A: 요즘 주말마다 스키장에 간다면서요?
B: 네. 제가 스키를 왜 이렇게 늦게 배웠는지 모르겠어요. 요즘 스키의 매력에 빠져 버렸어요.

ex A: 자막 없이 한국어로 드라마를 보는 게 어렵지 않아요?
B: 아니요. 드라마 내용도 재미있고 드라마를 보다가 배운 문법이 나오면 더 열심히 공부하고 싶어져요. 그래서 요즘 드라마를 보는 게 정말 즐거워요.
A: 드라마의 매력에 푹 빠졌군요.

ex A: 오늘 저녁에도 한강에 가려고요?
B: 네. 밤에 한강을 달리면 정말 시원하고 기분도 좋아지거든요. 요즘 제가 달리기의 매력에 푹 빠졌어요.

Dialogue

Lee Sora	Frank, what was your future dream when you were young?
Frank	I wanted to be a singer.
Lee Sora	A singer? That's really unexpected. Do you like to sing?
Frank	Yes. When I was young, I liked music. Then one day, I saw an opera and fell in love with music.
Lee Sora	I see. Then why didn't you keep studying music?
Frank	My voice broke when I was in middle school and I lost my motivation.
Lee Sora	That's too bad. Didn't you feel sorry when you gave up your dream?
Frank	Not at the time, but I sometimes regret it these days. If I hadn't given up back then, I might have become a famous singer.
Lee Sora	Why don't you join in a civic choir or singing club?
Frank	I'm interested in doing that, but I'm so busy with work that I don't have time for anything else.
Lee Sora	I see. By the way, being a chef suits you too.
Frank	Yes, I like cooking. It suits my temperament. But if I could go back to middle school, I think I would try to be a singer one more time.

Vocabulary & Expression

의미하다

의미하다 means ***to mean, to indicate***. It is used to inform or define what a certain word, writing, behavior, or phenomenon shows. A similar expression is 뜻하다.

ex A: 꿈에서 신발을 잃어버린다는 것은 어떤 의미예요?
B: 꿈에서 신발은 직장을 의미하기 때문에 신발을 잃어버리면 직장을 잃게 된다고 믿어요.

ex A: 저기 있는 사람들이 풀밭에서 뭘 그렇게 열심히 찾고 있어요?
B: 잎이 네 개 달린 클로버를 찾고 있는 거예요. 네 잎 클로버는 행운을 뜻하기 때문에 많은 사람들이 그걸 찾으면 행운이 온다고 믿거든요.

ex A: 한국의 유명한 민요인 '아리랑'에 나오는 '임'이 의미하는 것은 뭔가요?
B: '임'은 '사랑하는 님', 다시 말해 '사랑하는 사람'을 의미하는 것입니다. 사랑하는 사람이 떠나지 않길 바라는 마음을 표현한 노래지요.

영향을 미치다

영향을 미치다 means ***to have an effect, to influence***. It indicates having an effect or influence on something. Related expressions include 영향을 끼치다 and 영향을 주다.

ex A: 스마트폰이 사람들의 일상생활에 큰 영향을 미치고 있어요.
B: 맞아요. 이 작은 기계가 없었을 때는 사람들이 어떻게 살았는지 상상이 안 가네요.

ex A: 책이나 영화를 보는 게 사람들의 생각이나 사고방식에 큰 영향을 준다는 연구 결과가 있대요.
B: 그렇겠네요. 자신이 경험해 보지 못한 것도 책이나 영화를 통해서 알게 되고 생각해 볼 수 있기 때문인 것 같아요.

Reading Guide

This paragraph explains what is a good dream and what is a bad one and gives examples of both. Read it carefully, paying attention to the examples. (☞『이화 한국어 3-2』 p.70)

Answers

(1) 한자 '돈(豚)'과 화폐를 나타내는 '돈(money)'의 발음이 같기 때문이다.

(2) ④ Dreams can have different meanings depending on the dreamer's situation, and the same dream can be interpreted differently according to the society and culture concerned.

p.73

Vocabulary Expansion

헛– is placed in front of a noun or a verb to mean groundless, futile, useless, fruitless, or wrong.

헛수고
vain attempt

This means fruitless efforts or to go to such trouble.

ex A: 함께 가면 정말 좋을 텐데 영민 씨에게 같이 가자고 이야기해 보세요.
B: 이미 몇 번이나 말해 봤지만 헛수고였어요. 가기 싫대요.

헛걸음
fruitless trip

This means to come or go without accomplishing one's purpose.

ex 박물관이나 미술관에 가기 전에 휴일을 미리 알아두면 헛걸음하는 일이 없다.

헛소문
false rumor

This means a groundless and false rumor.

ex A: 최근에 영화 배우 김소희 씨가 우울증으로 고생하고 있대요.
B: 저도 그 뉴스 들었어요. 근거 없는 헛소문 때문에 상처 받는 연예인들이 많대요.

헛소리
nonsense

This means something said without substance, in sleep, or under the influence of liquor.

ex A: 이번 시합은 우리 편이 이길 게 분명해.
B: 헛소리하지 마. 우리 팀이 우승이야.

헛기침
clearing one's throat

This means to cough deliberately to clear one's throat, or to indicate one's presence.

ex 민호는 자신이 온 것을 알리기 위해 방문 앞에서 헛기침을 두어 번 하고 나서 방문을 열었다.

헛되다
to be wasted, to be fruitless, to be vain

This means that something is vain, without substance, or ungrounded and therefore hard to believe.

ex 운동선수들은 경기를 앞두고 지금까지의 노력들이 헛되지 않게 경기 전에 체력을 유지하는 것이 중요하다.

헛살다
to live in vain

This means to live without enjoying the things one deserves as a human being.

ex 자식들이 부모님을 잘 챙기지 않거나 모시려고 하지 않아서 인생을 헛살았다고 느끼는 부모님들이 많다.

헛디디다
to miss one's step

This means to slip or to lose one's footing.

ex A: 어쩌다 깁스를 했어? 다리를 다친 거야?
B: 응. 어제 계단을 내려가다가 헛디뎌서 넘어졌어.

Vocabulary Check

Part 1 준비합시다 01

- 가정하다 to suppose
- 타임머신 time machine
- 무인도 uninhabited island
- 투명인간 invisible man
- 멸망하다 to cease to exist, to go out of existence

Part 1 준비합시다 02

- 로봇 robot
- 화성 Mars
- 외계인 alien
- 올겨울 this winter
- 공통 commonness
- 통일되다 to be unified
- 우주여행 space travel

Part 1 들어 봅시다

- 순간 이동 teleportation
- 평균수명 average life expectancy
- 지구 earth
- 여유롭다 to be leisurely
- 북극 North Pole
- 빙하 iceberg, glacier
- 북극곰 polar bear
- 멸종하다 to become extinct

Part 1 말해 봅시다

- 당첨자 winner
- 사상 최고 record high
- 당첨금 payout, winnings
- 전액 total amount
- 대단하다 to be incredible
- 창업하다 to start a business
- 마련하다 to prepare
- 효녀 devoted/filial/good daughter
- 효도 filial duty
- 불행하다 to be unhappy

Part 2 준비합시다 01

- 성향 tendency
- 설문지 questionnaire, survey
- 차분하다 to be calm, to be relaxed
- 현실적 realistic, practical
- 미래지향적 future-oriented
- 상상력 imagination
- 기억나다 to remember

Part 2 준비합시다 02

- 깁스 cast

Part 2 들어 봅시다

- 태몽 conception dream
- 꿈을 꾸다 to have a dream
- 관련이 있다 to be related
- 살구 apricot
- 용 dragon
- 누렇다 (golden) yellow
- 백호 white tiger

Part 2 말해 봅시다

- 이루다 to accomplish
- 성악가 singer
- 변성기 break of voice
- 의욕 motivation
- 대회 competition, contest
- 소질 talent
- 체조 gymnastics

Part 3 읽어 봅시다

- 길몽 lucky/good dream
- 흉몽 ominous/bad dream
- 영상 picture, image
- 경우 case
- 조상 ancestor
- 화폐 currency
- 저금통 money box, coin bank
- 불길하다 to be ominous
- 영향을 미치다 to have an effect, to influence
- 해석되다 to be interpreted
- 그러므로 therefore
- 헛되다 to be vain, to be fruitless
- 정의 definition

Part 3 어휘를 늘려 봅시다

- 세차 car wash
- 웨딩드레스 wedding dress

Topic Vocabulary

Dream

- 목표를 이루다 to accomplish a goal
- 발전하다 to develop, to progress
- 열정 passion
- 장래희망 future dream, hopes
- 해몽 dream interpretation

 p.78

Grammar Focus

피동사(a passive verb) shows that the action performed by the subject is caused by another person or object, or that the subject is in a certain condition or state because of another person or object. 피동사 is made by attaching −이−, −히−, −리−, −기− to the stem of certain transitive verbs.

	Basic form	Passive verb	Basic form	Passive verb		Basic form	Passive verb	Basic form	Passive verb
이	놓다 묶다 바꾸다 보다	놓이다 묶이다 바뀌다 보이다	쌓다 섞다 쓰다 치다	쌓이다 섞이다 쓰이다 치이다	리	걸다 듣다 물다 밀다	걸리다 들리다 물리다 밀리다	열다 팔다 풀다 흔들다	열리다 팔리다 풀리다 흔들리다
히	닫다 막다 밟다	닫히다 막히다 밟히다	뽑다 잊다 잡다	뽑히다 잊히다 잡히다	기	끊다 담다 안다	끊기다 담기다 안기다	빼앗다 쫓다 찢다	빼앗기다 쫓기다 찢기다

ex A: 이번에 이사한 집은 전망이 어때?
B: 아주 좋아. 거실에서는 한강이 보이고 내 방에서는 남산이 보여.

ex A: 율리아 씨 책하고 제 책이 바뀐 것 같아요.
B: 어머, 미안해요. 제가 책을 잘못 가지고 간 것 같아요.

ex A: 아저씨, 요즘 어떤 과일이 잘 팔려요?
B: 날씨가 더워서 그런지 수박이 제일 많이 팔려요.

ex A: 어제 공원에서 산책하다가 모기에게 물렸어요. 너무 간지러워요.
B: 이 약을 발라 보세요. 간지럽지 않을 거예요.

ex A: 유키 씨, 왜 이렇게 늦게 왔어요?
B: 일찍 나왔는데 집 앞에서 교통사고가 나서 길이 아주 막혔어요.

ex A: 내 휴대 전화가 고장 난 것 같아. 통화 중에 갑자기 전화가 끊길 때가 많아.
B: 그래? 그럼 서비스 센터에 한번 가 봐.

Focus Plus

- Generally, passive verbs cannot be used in imperative or propositive sentences.

ex 조용한 음악을 들읍시다. (○)
조용한 음악이 들립시다. (×)

ex 안 좋은 일은 빨리 잊으세요. (○)
안 좋은 일이 빨리 잊히세요. (×)

- The sentence forms using passive verbs are as follows.

(1) 잡히다, 먹히다, 안기다, 읽히다, and 쫓기다 are often used in the following sentence form.

N1이/가	N2을/를	V
경찰이	도둑을	잡아요

→

N2이/가	N1에게	Passive verb
도둑이	경찰에게	잡혀요

(2) 열리다, 끊기다, 들리다, 막히다, 바뀌다, 보이다, and 잠기다 are often used in the following sentence form.

N1을/를	V
창문을	열어요

→

N1이/가	Passive verb
창문이	열려요

(3) 걸리다, 꽂히다, 놓이다, 쌓이다, and 쓰이다 are used in the following sentence form.

N1이/가	N2에	V
옷을	옷장에	걸어요

→

N2이/가	N2에	Passive verb
옷이	옷장에	걸려 있어요

- Among the verbs with –이–, –히–, –리–, –기– attached, some passive and causative verbs have the same forms. (See 『이화 한국어 3–1』 Chapter 4, p.78)

  ex A: 저 멀리 보이는 풍경이 정말 아름답지 않아요? (passive verb)
  B: 그러네요. 아름다운 풍경을 보니 마음까지 편안해지네요.

  ex A: 어제 선생님이 이번 문화수업에서 찍은 사진을 보여 주셨어. (causative verb)
  B: 그래? 나도 보여 달라고 부탁 드려야겠다.

- Verbs without –이–, –히–, –리–, –기– attached to them can be given passive meaning by attaching –아/어지다. (See 『이화 한국어 3–2』 Chapter 9, p.38)

  ex A: 옷에 볼펜이 묻었는데 잘 지워지지 않아요. 어떻게 하죠?
  B: 그럴 때는 알코올로 지워 보세요.

- The verb form N하다, such as 운동하다 and 청소하다, can be changed to N당하다, N되다 (See 『이화 한국어 3–2』 Chapter 9, p.53), and N받다 (See 『이화 한국어 3–2』 Chapter 11, p.93) to show passive meaning.

  ex A: 영민 씨가 수진 씨한테 데이트 신청을 했는데 거절당했대요.
  B: 정말이에요? 전 수진 씨가 영민 씨한테 관심이 있는 줄 알았는데요.

  ex A: 여기는 무엇을 하는 곳인가요?
  B: 이곳은 학생들이 수업이 없는 시간에 와서 공부를 하거나 쉬는 곳으로 사용되고 있습니다.

  ex A: 저는 '은수'라는 이름 때문에 가끔 남자로 오해받을 때가 있어요.
  B: '수'자로 끝나는 이름이 남자 이름인 경우가 많아서 그럴 거예요.

Answers

어떤 사람의 가방을 훔친 도둑이 신호등이 바뀌지 않았는데 횡단보도를 그냥 건넜어요. 그러다가 빨간색 오토바이에 치였어요. 그런데 경찰과 경찰견에게 쫓기던 도둑은 그대로 도망갔어요. 그렇지만 곧 경찰견에게 다리를 물렸어요. 그래서 그 도둑은 결국 경찰에게 잡혔어요.

Grammar Focus

-아/어 놓다 means to maintain or attempt to maintain the condition following completion of a certain action. It is attached to a verb.

Basic form	-아/어 놓다	Basic form	-아/어 놓다
세우다	세워 놓다	만들다	만들어 놓다
차리다	차려 놓다	틀다	틀어 놓다
정리하다	정리해 놓다	짓다	지어 놓다
접다	접어 놓다	고르다	골라 놓다

ex A: 우리 이번 주말에 영화를 보러 갈까요?
B: 네, 좋아요. 제가 오늘 저녁에 예매해 놓을게요.

ex A: 밖은 아주 더운데 교실에 들어오니까 시원하네요.
B: 마이클 씨가 일찍 와서 에어컨을 켜 놓아서 그럴 거예요.

ex A: 교실에서 밥을 먹은 후에는 꼭 환기를 시키세요.
B: 그럴게요. 한 10분 정도 창문을 열어 놓으면 될까요?

ex A: 밥 먹으러 빨리 가요. 점심시간이라 사람이 많을 거예요.
B: 천천히 가도 돼요. 후배가 미리 가서 주문해 놓는다고 했어요.

ex A: 책을 다 읽은 후에는 꼭 제자리에 꽂아 놓으세요.
B: 네, 선생님. 정리해 놓을게요.

Focus Plus

- When -아/어 놓다 is used with -아/어서, -아/어(요) or -았/었어(요), it can be contracted to -아/어 놔서, -아/어 놔요, or -아/어 놨어요.

ex A: 여기 어디 젖은 옷을 말릴 만한 곳이 있어?
B: 여기에 걸어 놔. 햇볕이 잘 들어서 금방 마를 거야.

Answers

① A: 제이슨 씨, 생일 파티 준비 다 했어요?
B: 아니요. 풍선은 불어 놓았는데
아직 풍선으로 장식하지 못했어요.
파티 시작하기 전까지 장식해 놓을게요.

② A: 왕치엔 씨, 생일 파티 준비 다 했어요?
B: 아니요. 생일 카드는 준비해 놓았는데
아직 피자는 주문하지 못했어요.
파티 시작하기 전까지 주문해 놓을게요.

③ A: 마리 씨, 생일 파티 준비 다 했어요?
B: 아니요. 선물은 사 놓았는데 아직 포장하지 못했어요.
파티 시작하기 전까지 포장해 놓을게요.

④ A: 아키라 씨, 생일 파티 준비 다 했어요?
B: 아니요. 샐러드는 만들어 놓았는데
아직 그릇에 담지 못했어요.
파티 시작하기 전까지 담아 놓을게요.

⑤ A: 하오밍 씨, 생일 파티 준비 다 했어요?
B: 아니요. '생일 축하합니다'라고 벽에 써서
붙여 놓았는데 아직 음료수를 준비하지 못했어요.
파티 시작하기 전까지 음료수를 준비해 놓을게요.

Vocabulary & Expression

우르르

우르르 means ***with a crash, in a heap***. It indicates the sound or appearance of things that are piled up suddenly collapsing or falling.

ex A: 아니 어쩌다가 이 그릇들이 다 깨졌어요?
B: 선반 위에 올려둔 상자들이 우르르 쏟아지는 바람에 선반 아래 있던 그릇들이 다 깨졌어요.

Script

(1) Announcer Can you introduce this week's bestsellers?

Reporter Yes. Here, I have this week's top 10 bestsellers. Among them, this one is the bestselling book this week. It made headlines when it hit sales of one million copies. Actually, it was written 5 years ago and at that time, no one paid much attention to it. But when it was recently made into a movie, it started to attract attention again.

(2) Announcer The Architecture of the Year Award has been decided. Can you please tell us about it?

Reporter Yes. The building right here has been selected as this year's most beautiful work of architecture. It was built in March and is the work of the famous architect Kim Yeongsu.

Announcer Kim received another award a few years ago, didn't he?

Reporter Yes, that's right. Kim is recognized as one of Korea's greatest architects. He's famous for functional buildings, and this award winning work is impressive for these spaces where people can appreciate nature. In contrast to other works, it is highly acclaimed for its harmony with the natural setting.

(3) Announcer Yesterday there was an earthquake in the suburbs of Seoul?

Reporter Yes. The earthquake lasted about 3 seconds and caused apartments to shake and things to collapse. The damage was minor, but the residents seem to be shocked. Let's hear from one of them.

Resident Yesterday, my family was in the living room together and suddenly we heard a crashing sound. Then the living room floor shook. We were shocked, because we had never experienced an earthquake before. But we are so lucky that it didn't do much damage.

Reporter Having experienced this earthquake, it seems the residents feel that Korea is not safe from earthquakes.

Answers

(1) ④ This book received attention again when it was recently made into a movie.

(2) ② The announcer and reporter are talking about the work of Kim Yeongsu, which received the Architecture of the Year Award.

(3) ④ After the residents heard a crashing sound, they saw the living room shake.

Vocabulary & Expression

한잠도 못 자다

한잠도 못 자다 means ***to not sleep at all***. This indicates one does not sleep even for a moment. Similar expressions are 한숨도 못 자다, 밤새 눈을 붙이지 못하다, and 뜬눈으로 밤을 지새우다.

ex A: 아침부터 무슨 커피를 두 잔이나 마셔요?
B: 부장님께 오늘까지 제출해야 할 서류를 완성하느라고 밤새 한잠도 못 잤거든요.

가슴이 두근거리다

가슴이 두근거리다 means ***one's heart pounds***. This indicates that one's heart beats fast with amazement or excitement. Similar expressions are 가슴이 두근두근하다 and 심장이 두근거리다.

ex A: 아까 본 영화 정말 무섭지 않았어요?
B: 네. 무서운 장면이 나올 때마다 가슴이 두근거려서 혼났어요.

Dialogue

Park Yeongmin	Jason, you look so tired this morning. Did you stay up all night at work?
Jason	Yes. I didn't get any sleep at all.
Park Yeongmin	Why? Did something happen?
Jason	I left the office around midnight, after catching up on some work.
Park Yeongmin	And?
Jason	On my way to the elevator, I heard a strange sound. But I couldn't see anything because the lights in the hallway were all off. So I just got in the elevator and when it reached the 4th floor, it suddenly started to shake.
Park Yeongmin	So, what happened?
Jason	I heard the strange sound again. Then the elevator suddenly stopped and all the lights in the elevator went out.
Park Yeongmin	Why didn't you call someone for help?
Jason	When I took my phone out to call someone, I dropped it and it broke. So I had no choice but to stay in the dark elevator all night, hearing that strange sound until dawn.
Park Yeongmin	You must have been terrified. Are you all right now?
Jason	Don't even talk about it. When I think about last night, my heart still pounds.

Grammar Focus

–(으)니까 means that one finds out or realizes a new fact after he/she has done something. It is attached to a verb and can be contracted to –(으)니.

Basic form	–(으)니까	Basic form	–(으)니까
보다	보니까	입다	입으니까
가다	가니까	듣다	들으니까
먹다	먹으니까	만들다	만드니까

ex A: 어제 왜 전화 안 했어? 잠도 안 자고 기다렸는데.
B: 미안. 어젯밤에 집에 들어가니까 12시가 넘어서 전화 못 했어.

ex A: 아까 선생님이 찾으시던데 선생님 만났어요?
B: 아니요. 선생님이 찾으신다고 해서 교실에 가니까 안 계시던데요.

ex A: 오랜만에 동창회를 하니까 못 만났던 친구들 얼굴도 보고 참 좋다.
B: 그러게. 우리 앞으로는 자주 모이자.

ex A: 웬일로 치마를 입고 왔어? 치마는 불편해서 싫다고 했잖아?
B: 불편할 줄 알았는데 막상 입으니까 그렇게 불편하지 않네.

ex A: 아직도 이 문제의 답을 모르겠어요?
B: 선생님의 설명을 들으니까 이제 알겠어요.

ex A: 이 떡볶이 정말 줄리아 씨가 혼자서 만들었어요?
B: 네. 만드는 방법이 복잡할 줄 알았는데 실제로 만들어 보니까 그렇게 어렵지 않아요. 율리아 씨도 한번 만들어 보세요.

Focus Plus

- –(으)니까, which means to find out or to realize a new fact, cannot be used with –았/었– or –겠–. In addition, –겠– or –(으)ㄹ 것이다 cannot be used in the clause following –(으)니까.

ex 어제 한강에 가니까 사람이 많았다. (○)
어제 한강에 갔으니까 사람이 많았다. (×)
내일 약국에 가겠으니까 약이 없다. (×)
내일 약국에 가니까 약이 없을 것이다. (×)

- –(으)니까, which means to find out or realize a new fact, is often attached to –아/어 보다 and used in the form –아/어 보니까 .

ex A: 아까 신어 본 신발을 왜 안 샀어요?
B: 보기에는 예쁜데 신어 보니까 발이 너무 아파서요.

ex A: 지난 방학에 회사에서 인턴을 했다면서요. 어땠어요?
B: 제가 직접 회사에서 일해 보니까 돈 버는 게 진짜 어렵다는 것을 알겠어요.

- –(으)니까 is also used when the preceding content is the reason or grounds for judging the following content. (See 『이화 한국어 2–1』 Chapter 5, p.100) In this case, –(으)니까 can be used with –았/었– or –겠–, while –겠– or –(으)ㄹ 것이다 can be used in the clause following –(으)니까.

ex A: 내일 율리아 씨 생일인데 무슨 선물을 사면 좋을지 모르겠어요.
B: 율리아 씨는 액세서리를 좋아하니까 귀걸이를 선물하는 게 어때요?

ex A: 우리 이번 주말에는 어떤 영화를 볼까요?
B: 지난 번에는 무서운 영화를 봤으니까 이번에는 좀 재미있고 웃기는 영화를 보면 어때요?

ex A: 손님, 아무래도 이 노트북 고치는 데 일주일 이상 걸릴 것 같은데요?
B: 다음 주까지는 못 기다리겠으니까 이번 주까지는 꼭 고쳐 주세요.

ex A: 고등학교 때 제일 친했던 친구가 오늘 한국에 와요. 그래서 공항에 마중하러 나가요.
B: 그래요? 오랜만에 만나니까 정말 반갑겠어요.

ex A: 내일이 드디어 시험 보는 날이에요. 너무 긴장이 돼요.
B: 그동안 열심히 공부했으니까 꼭 합격할 거예요. 걱정하지 마세요.

- –(으)니까 can be used in the form –(으)니까는 or –(으)니깐 by adding the postposition 는 to emphasize the meaning.

ex A: 떡볶이가 너무 매워 보여요.
B: 보기에는 그런데 막상 먹어 보니깐 생각보다 맵지 않고 맛있어요. 수진 씨도 한번 먹어 봐요.

ex A: 우리 버스 타고 갈까요?
B: 지금은 퇴근 시간이라 차가 막히니깐 지하철을 타고 갑시다.

Answers

① A: 며칠 전에 지하철을 탔다면서요? 어땠어요?
B: 지하철을 타니까 젊은 사람들은 노약자석에 앉지 않던데요.

② A: 어제 삼계탕을 먹어 봤다면서요? 어땠어요?
B: 삼계탕을 먹어 보니까 더위에 지친 여름에 먹는 이유를 알겠어요.

③ A: 한국 대학생을 만나 봤다면서요? 어땠어요?
B: 네. 한국 대학생을 만나 보니까 취업 때문에 고민이 많던데요.

④ A: 한국 소설을 읽어 봤다면서요? 어땠어요?
B: 네. 한국 소설을 읽어 보니까 어려운 단어가 많지만 한국어 공부에 도움이 될 것 같았어요.

⑤ A: 주말에 콘서트에 갔었다면서요? 어땠어요?
B: 가수의 노래를 공연장에서 직접 들으니까 텔레비전에서 볼 때보다 더 감동적이었어요.

Grammar Focus

-아/어 있다 means that a condition is maintained after a certain action has been completed. Since it is attached only to a verb that does not need objects, it is often attached to a passive verb or a verb that has a passive meaning such as -아/어지다.

Basic form	-아/어 있다	Basic form	-아/어 있다
서다	서 있다	쌓이다	쌓여 있다
걸리다	걸려 있다	잠기다	잠겨 있다
닫히다	닫혀 있다	켜지다	켜져 있다

ex A: 직원들이 모두 퇴근한 것 같아요.
사무실 불이 꺼져 있어요.
B: 그래요? 그런데 문은 안 잠겨 있어요. 이상하네요.

ex A: 교실이 왜 이렇게 추워요?
B: 창문이 열려 있었나 봐요.
제가 창문을 닫을게요.

ex A: 여기가 김 선생님 사무실이 맞지?
B: 응, 맞는 것 같아. 그런데 문 앞에 지금 회의 중이라고 쓰여 있어. 조금 후에 다시 오자.

Focus Plus

- When an honorific expression is needed for the subject, -아/어 계시다 is used instead of -아/어 있다.

ex A: 마이클 씨, 할아버지 건강은 좀 좋아지셨어요?
B: 지금도 별로 안 좋으세요. 아직도 병원에 입원해 계세요.

- While -아/어 있다 means that the condition or result is maintained after a certain action is completed, -고 있다 (See 「이화 한국어 1-2」 Chapter 9, p.38) means that a certain action is in progress.

ex A: 영민 씨가 어제부터 안 보이네요. 영민 씨 어디 갔어요?
B: 내일 열리는 회의를 준비하기 위해서 지금 부산에 가 있어요.

ex A: 제이슨 씨, 지금 어디세요? 저는 도착했어요.
B: 미안해요. 버스를 놓쳐서 지금 택시 타고 가고 있어요. 조금만 기다려 주세요.

Answers

침대 위에는 곰 인형이 놓여 있습니다. 곰 인형 옆에는 강아지가 앉아 있습니다. 침대 왼쪽 벽에는 메모판이 걸려 있습니다. 메모판에는 메모지가 붙어 있습니다. 메모지에는 메모가 쓰여 있습니다. 방 오른쪽에는 책상이 놓여 있습니다. 책상 위에는 컴퓨터가 놓여 있습니다. 컴퓨터는 꺼져 있습니다. 컴퓨터 옆에는 스탠드가 켜져 있습니다. 스탠드와 컴퓨터 사이에 책 두 권이 쌓여 있습니다. 책상 왼쪽에는 책장이 있습니다. 책장 안에는 책이 꽂혀 있고 액자도 놓여 있습니다. 그리고 서랍은 닫혀 있습니다. 책상 앞에는 의자가 있습니다. 책상 오른쪽 옆에는 옷이 걸려 있습니다. 옷 아래에는 바구니가 있습니다. 바구니 안에는 수건이 들어 있습니다. 방 가운데에는 탁자가 있습니다. 탁자 위에는 꽃병이 놓여 있습니다. 꽃병에는 꽃이 꽂혀 있습니다. 탁자 아래에는 카펫이 깔려 있습니다. 방에 창문이 하나 있습니다. 창문에는 블라인드가 내려져 있습니다. 창문 오른쪽 옆에 액자가 걸려 있습니다. 액자에는 그림이 그려져 있습니다.

PART2 들어 봅시다 목격한 사고 현장에 대한 대화 듣기

p.86

Vocabulary & Expression

사고를 당하다

사고를 당하다 means ***to have/get into an accident***. It indicates meeting with an accident and receiving damage as a result. 당하다 is often used for a situation in which one personally experiences something unfortunate.

ex A: 배우 김진수가 다쳤다는 기사 봤어?
B: 응. 영화를 찍다가 말에서 떨어지는 사고를 당했대.

어쨌든

어쨌든 means ***anyway***. It is used to emphasize one's thoughts or the present situation, regardless of any preceding situation. Similar expressions are 아무튼 and 하여튼.

ex A: 죄송합니다. 중요한 전화가 와서 꼭 받을 수밖에 없었어요.
B: 어쨌든 운전 중에 휴대 전화를 사용하는 건 법규를 위반하신 거니까 벌금을 내셔야 합니다.

Script

Policeman	Are you the one who was at the scene of the traffic accident last Friday?
Mari	Yes, I was there.
Policeman	Can you explain what you saw that day, in detail?
Mari	The street was slippery because there was so much snow on the ground. There was almost nobody around, since it was just a little bit after 6 a.m. I was walking toward the front entrance of school when I heard a thud. So I looked back, and there was a female student who had collapsed on the ground. There was a red car standing in front of her, and it seemed that she had been hit by the car.
Policeman	Did you see the license plate?
Mari	No, I didn't.
Policeman	Did you see the driver by any chance?
Mari	Of course. As soon as the accident happened, the driver got out and took the girl to the car.
Policeman	What did the driver look like?
Mari	She was wearing a black suit and appeared to be in her early thirties. I thought she was going to take the student to the hospital. Did anything happen to her?
Policeman	No. The driver took the student to the hospital and disappeared. Anyway, thank you for your cooperation.

Answers

(1) ③ This man is a policeman. He is asking the eyewitness about the accident last Friday.

(2) ① The accident happened a little after 6:00 a.m. on Friday, not in the evening.

(3) ③ The driver took the student to the hospital and disappeared.

Vocabulary & Expression

자국이 나다

자국이 나다 means ***to have a mark appear***. This indicates that a mark or stain is left on something through contact with another object, or that the trace of change has been left by something, altering the original condition.

ex A: 인터넷 쇼핑몰에서 가방을 샀는데 아무래도 누가 사용한 적이 있는 물건 같아요. 가방 여기저기에 긁힌 자국이 나 있고 먼지도 많이 묻어 있어요.
B: 그러면 얼른 교환해 달라고 하세요.

엉망이 되다

엉망이 되다 means ***to become a mess, to be ruined***. This indicates that a work or object becomes a mess or hectic and disordered. A similar expression is 엉망진창이 되다.

ex A: 책상 위에 커피를 쏟아서 책이랑 공책이랑 다 엉망이 됐어요. 시험이 얼마 안 남았는데 어떻게 하지요?
B: 일단 제 책하고 공책 빌려줄게요. 제 책하고 공책으로 공부해요.

Dialogue

Policeman	Did you notify the police that you had been robbed?
Akira	Yes. When I came back home around at 7 p.m. today, the door was open and everything was a mess inside.
Policeman	What was stolen?
Akira	The laptop on the desk and some cash in the desk drawer.
Policeman	Is that all that was stolen, the laptop and cash?
Akira	The suit that was hanging in the closet over there is also gone.
Policeman	Then, is there anything that has changed?
Akira	Look at the refrigerator over there. When I left home this morning the door was closed, but when I came back, it was open.
Policeman	I see. Was the window over there broken?
Akira	Yes. When I came in, the window was broken like that. And it seems the thief came inside with his shoes on. There were footprints on the floor.
Policeman	Do you suspect anyone?
Achira	Well, I don't know because I only moved to this town recently.
Policeman	All right. We will investigate the matter.

Vocabulary & Expression

리본이 달리다

리본이 달리다 means ***to have a ribbon tied (on something).*** 달리다 means that something is hung, tied up, or installed at a certain location. 달리다 is the passive form of 달다.

ex A: 저기 저 리본이 달린 원피스 어때요? 저한테 어울릴 것 같아요?
B: 색깔도 예쁘고 디자인도 괜찮은데요. 한번 입어 보세요.

평생

평생 means ***one's whole life.*** A similar expression is 일생.

ex A: 남자 친구가 뭐라고 하며 청혼했어요?
B: 나와 평생을 함께 하고 싶다고 했어요.

깜짝 파티를 준비해 놓지 않았을까 하는 기대를 하다

깜짝 파티를 준비해 놓지 않았을까 하는 기대를 하다 means ***to anticipate the preparation of a surprise party.*** This indicates that one expects a surprise party to be held under the assumption that a surprise party has been prepared. –(으)ㄹ까 하는 기대를 하다 can also be used to show one's anticipation for something that is likely to happen.

ex A: 어제 야구 경기 봤어요? 우리 팀이 너무 아쉽게 졌어요.
B: 저도 이번에는 이기지 않을까 하는 기대를 했는데. 아쉬워요.

ex A: 이번에 면접 본 회사에서는 연락이 왔어요?
B: 아직 안 왔어요. 이메일을 열어 볼 때마다 연락이 오지 않았을까 하고 기대를 하는데 연락이 없네요.

Reading Guide

This passage is written about an unforgettable day. Read it carefully and think about how the day was, where the writer went, what kind of place it was, what happened there, and why it became an unforgettable day. (☞『이화 한국어 3-2』 p.90.)

Answers

(1) ③ The most unforgettable day for this person was the day her boyfriend proposed to her a few years ago.

(2) ④ The pretty lights were shining, hung not around the table but on the door of the restaurant.

Vocabulary Expansion

—받다, when attached to some nouns, turns the nouns into verbs with passive meaning.

진찰받다
to have a checkup

ex A: 요즘 계속 머리가 아파서 일 주일째 두통약을 매일 먹고 있어요.
B: 그렇게 약만 먹으면 안 돼요. 빨리 병원에 가서 의사에게 진찰받아 봐요.

칭찬받다
to receive praise

ex A: 이번 워크숍에서 발표 잘했다고 교수님께 칭찬받았어요.
B: 그동안 고생한 보람이 있네요.

ex A: 이번에 장학금을 받았다면서요? 정말 기분 좋겠어요?
B: 네. 장학금 받은 것도 좋지만 부모님하고 선생님께 칭찬받은 게 더 기분 좋아요.

사랑받다
to be loved

ex A: 수진 씨, 혹시 '김소월'이라는 시인 알아요?
B: 그럼요. 한국 사람들에게서 가장 사랑받는 시인이에요.

존경받다
to be respected

ex A: 한국인들에게 가장 존경받는 사람이 누구예요?
B: 아마 세종대왕과 이순신 장군일 거예요.

인정받다
to be recognized

ex A: 요즘 외국에서도 김치를 좋아하는 사람들이 많다고 해요.
B: 네. 김치는 맛도 있지만 건강에도 아주 좋은 음식으로 인정받고 있어요. 특히 암 예방에 좋은 식품으로 주목받고 있어요.

소개받다
to be introduced

ex A: 제이슨 씨, 아내가 한국분이라면서요? 두 분이 어떻게 만나셨어요?
B: 회사 동료한테서 소개받았어요. 처음 보자마자 첫눈에 반했어요.

ex A: 마이클 씨는 저희 언어교육원을 어떻게 알게 되었어요?
B: 한국어를 정말 잘 배울 수 있는 곳이라고 친구에게서 소개받았어요.

안내받다
to be guided

ex A: 이 스포츠 센터의 운동 프로그램에 대해서 알고 싶은데 어디로 가야 하나요?
B: 저쪽에 가시면 저희 직원한테 자세하게 안내받으실 수 있습니다.

평가받다
to be evaluated

ex A: 이건 제가 잘 모르는 회사 제품인데 품질이 괜찮을까요?
B: 손님, 이 회사는 작은 회사지만 품질만은 대기업보다 더 우수한 걸로 평가받는 회사예요. 믿고 사셔도 괜찮을 것 같습니다.

Vocabulary Check

Part 1 준비합시다 01

- 열리다 to be open
- 막히다 to be blocked
- 팔리다 to be sold
- 쌓이다 to be piled up
- 끊기다 to be cut off
- 도망가다 to run away
- 잡히다 to be caught
- 현장 site, scene
- 목격하다 to witness
- 들리다 to be heard
- 치이다 to be hit/run over
- 쫓기다 to be chased
- 물리다 to be bitten
- 비명 소리 scream
- 피해 damage
- 흔들리다 to be shaken
- 주민 resident
- 우르르 with a crash

Part 1 준비합시다 02

- (상을) 차리다 to set the table
- 장식하다 to decorate
- 포장하다 to pack
- 담다 to put something in
- 붙이다 to attach, to paste

Part 1 들어 봅시다

- 금주 this week
- 화제 topic
- 쓰이다 to be written
- 읽히다 to be read
- 건축가 architect
- 건축상 architecture award
- 대표적 representative
- 뽑히다 to be selected, to be chosen
- 실용적 functional, practical
- 평가를 받다 to be evaluated
- 근교 suburb

Part 1 말해 봅시다

- 사건 accident, case
- 밤을 새우다 to stay up all night
- 일이 밀리다 to have work piled up
- (전화가) 걸리다 to have a call made
- 신호가 가다 to have the phone ring
- 혼나다 to be scolded
- 끔찍하다 to be terrible
- 소름이 끼치다 to get goose bumps
- 한잠도 못 자다 to get no sleep at all
- 복도 hallway, aisle

Part 2 준비합시다 01

- 국제결혼 international marriage
- 정 affection
- 재래시장 traditional market
- 흥정하다 to bargain
- 지치다 to be worn out by

Part 1 준비합시다 02

- 놓이다 to be placed
- 입원하다 to be hospitalized
- 닫히다 to be closed
- 꽂히다 to be put
- 걸리다 to be hung
- 깔리다 to be spread
- 내려지다 to be pulled down

Part 1 들어 봅시다

- 사고를 당하다 to have an accident

- 조사하다 to investigate, to look into
- 옮기다 to move
- 일어나다 to happen, to occur
- 사고를 내다 to cause an accident

Part 2 말해 봅시다

- 도둑맞다 to have (a thing) stolen
- 신고 notification
- 도둑이 들다 to get robbed
- 서랍 drawer
- 선반 shelf
- 자국이 나다 to have a mark appear
- 엉망이 되다 to become a mess
- 의심이 가다 to be suspicious

Part 3 읽어 봅시다

- 기억에 남다 to remain in one's memory
- 청혼을 받다 to be proposed to
- 약도 map
- (리본이) 달리다 (a ribbon) to be tied up
- 평생 lifetime
- 기대를 하다 to expect, to anticipate

Part 3 어휘를 늘려 봅시다

- 큰 상 big prize
- 여행 상품 travel product

Topic Vocabulary

Accident

- 재난을 당하다 to experience a disaster
- 심하게 비바람이 불다 to be harshly windy and rainy
- 태풍이 불다 to have a storm come
- 폭우가 내리다 to have heavy rainfall
- 폭설이 내리다 to have heavy snowfall
- 물난리가 나다 to suffer from a flood
- 홍수가 나다 to get flooded
- 지진이 일어나다 to have an earthquake occur
- 불이 나다 to have a fire break out
- 화재가 일어나다 to have a fire break out
- 차에 치이다 to get hit by a car
- 교통사고가 나다 to have a traffic accident
- 다른 차와 부딪히다 to bump into another car
- 접촉 사고가 나다 to collide with another car
- 도둑을 잡다 to catch a thief
- 소매치기를 당하다 to have one's pocket picked
- 사고를 신고하다 to report an accident
- 사고를 목격하다 to witness an accident
- 범인을 쫓다 to pursue/chase a criminal
- 범인을 잡다 to catch a criminal

PART1 준비합시다 01 • –았/었으면 좋겠다

p.98

Grammar Focus

–았/었으면 좋겠다 is used to express one's hopes or wishes for something to happen in the future. It also suggests that the one's wishes are different to the actual situation.

Basic form	–았/었으면 좋겠다	Basic form	–았/었으면 좋겠다
크다	컸으면 좋겠다	가다	갔으면 좋겠다
많다	많았으면 좋겠다	붙다	붙었으면 좋겠다
길다	길었으면 좋겠다	걷다	걸었으면 좋겠다
쉽다	쉬웠으면 좋겠다	짓다	지었으면 좋겠다

ex A: 저는 발이 작아서 신발을 사기가 너무 힘들어요. 발이 좀 컸으면 좋겠어요.
B: 그래요? 저는 발이 커서 좀 작았으면 좋겠는데.

ex A: 종강이 다가오니까 과제에다가 시험까지 있어서 할 게 너무 많아.
B: 그러게 말이야. 정말 하루만 신나게 놀았으면 좋겠어.

ex A: 내일 회사 면접시험 본다고 했지? 행운을 빌어.
B: 고마워. 이번에는 꼭 붙었으면 좋겠어.

ex A: 올해 여름도 작년 여름만큼 더울까요?
B: 글쎄요. 올해는 작년보다 좀 덜 더웠으면 좋겠는데.

Focus Plus

- The expression –았/었으면 좋겠다 can be substituted with –았/었으면 하다 or –았/었으면 싶다.

ex 오늘 몸이 조금 안 좋아서 일찍 퇴근했으면 좋겠습니다.
(= 일찍 퇴근했으면 합니다)
(= 일찍 퇴근했으면 싶습니다)

Answers

① A: 박영민 씨, 새해에 바라는 것 있어요?
B: 네. 출퇴근 시간이 많이 걸려서 회사 근처로 이사했으면 좋겠어요.

② A: 유키 씨, 새해에 바라는 것 있어요?
B: 네. 가족들 얼굴을 오랫동안 못 봐서 고향에 다녀왔으면 좋겠어요.

③ A: 아키라 씨, 새해에 바라는 것 있어요?
B: 네. 작년에 회계사 시험에 떨어졌는데 올해에는 꼭 시험에 붙었으면 좋겠어요.

④ A: 율리아 씨, 새해에 바라는 것 있어요?
B: 네. 저는 아들만 있는데 올해는 꼭 딸을 낳았으면 좋겠어요.

⑤ A: 마리 씨, 새해에 바라는 것 있어요?
B: 네. 어머니가 좀 편찮으신데 올해는 어머니가 건강해지셨으면 좋겠어요.

Grammar Focus

When -(으)ㄴ/는지 is used with interrogative words such as 얼마나 or 어찌나, it emphasizes the considerable degree or level of the situation aforementioned. 얼마나/어찌나 -(으)ㄴ/는지 is typically used to emphasize the expression 아주 -아/어서. To stress the considerable degree or level of a past situation, the expression 얼마나/어찌나 -았/었는지 is used.

Basic form	-(으)ㄴ/는지	-았/었는지
크다	큰지	컸는지
같다	같은지	같았는지
덥다	더운지	더웠는지
받다	받는지	받았는지
공부하다	공부하는지	공부했는지
묻다	묻는지	물었는지

ex A: 어제도 늦게까지 일했는데 피곤하지 않았어요?
B: 얼마나 피곤한지 집에 가자마자 옷도 안 벗고 잤어요.

ex A: 아키라 씨, 살이 많이 빠졌네요.
B: 네. 지난주에 감기 때문에 어찌나 아팠는지 밥을 못 먹어서 살이 3kg이나 빠졌어요.

ex A: 지난주에 놀이공원에 갔다 왔다면서요? 재미있었어요?
B: 어찌나 사람이 많았는지 놀이기구를 탈 때마다 한 시간 이상 기다렸어요.

ex A: 이렇게 더운 날에 밖에서 운동을 했어요? 덥지 않았어요?
B: 얼마나 더웠는지 땀으로 옷이 다 젖었어요.

ex A: 유키 씨는 공부를 정말 열심히 하는 것 같아요.
B: 그러게요. 얼마나 열심히 공부하는지 식사 시간에도 책을 옆에 놓고 읽으면서 밥을 먹더라고요.

ex A: 추석에 고향 잘 다녀왔어요? 고속도로에 차가 많아서 복잡하지 않았어요?
B: 네. 차가 어찌나 막히는지 서울에서 부산까지 가는 데 8시간이나 걸렸어요.

ex A: 오늘 친구 생일파티에 다녀온다고 했지? 저녁은 잘 먹었니?
B: 네. 음식이 정말 맛있었어요. 얼마나 많이 먹었는지 내일까지 배부를 것 같아요.

ex A: 우산이 없었어요? 옷이 다 젖었네요.
B: 비가 얼마나 많이 오는지 우산을 써도 별 소용이 없었어요.

ex A: 어제 율리아 씨가 수업 시간에 노래를 불렀다면서요?
B: 네. 노래를 어찌나 잘하는지 가수보다 더 잘하는 것 같았어요.

Focus Plus

- 얼마나/어찌나 -(으)ㄴ/는지 is used to emphasize the considerable degree or level of a situation that is under way, while 얼마나/어찌나 -(으)ㄹ지 is used to express the considerable degree or level of a situation yet to come.

ex A: 오늘도 이화 식당에서 밥을 먹을 거예요?
B: 네. 그 식당 음식이 어찌나 맛있는지 매일 가게 되네요.

ex A: 내일 모임은 명동에 있는 식당에서 한대요.
얼마 전 텔레비전에서 맛집으로 소개된 식당이래요.
B: 그래요? 음식이 얼마나 맛있을지 기대가 되네요.

- A sentence can end with 얼마나/어찌나 -(으)ㄴ/는지, without a following clause.

ex A: 학교 앞에 새로 생긴 옷 가게에 그렇게 사람이 많다면서?
B: 50% 세일을 한다고 해서 나도 어제 가 봤는데 얼마나 사람이 많은지.

ex A: 밖에 아직도 눈이 많이 내려요?
B: 네, 엄청 많이 내려요. 게다가 바람까지 어찌나 부는지.

- 얼마나 -(으)ㄴ/는지 can be used to ask about an unknown situation or to express uncertainty about a situation.

ex A: 식당 밖에서 기다리는 손님들이 얼마나 많은지 확인해 봤어요?
B: 한 열 명 정도 기다리고 있는 것 같아요.

ex A: 회사 앞에 새로 생긴 식당이 맛있다던데 우리 이번 회식은 거기에서 합시다.
B: 다른 사람들 말만으론 실제로 음식이 얼마나 맛있는지 알 수 없잖아요.
우리가 한번 먼저 먹어 봅시다.

Answers

① A: 이번에 새로 들어간 회사 다닐 만해요?
B: 아니요. 어찌나 해외 출장이 잦은지 시차에 적응하기가 힘들어요.

② A: 이번에 새로 들어간 회사 다닐 만해요?
B: 아니요. 고객들이 어찌나 까다로운지 고객 상대하기가 어려워요.

③ A: 이번에 새로 들어간 회사 다닐 만해요?
B: 아니요. 출근 시간이 어찌나 이른지 매일 새벽같이 출근해요.

④ A: 이번에 새로 들어간 회사 다닐 만해요?
B: 아니요. 어찌나 퇴근길이 막히는지 도로에서 낭비하는 시간이 많아요.

⑤ A: 이번에 새로 들어간 회사 다닐 만해요?
B: 아니요. 어찌나 월급이 적은지 저축할 돈이 없어요.

p.100

Vocabulary & Expression

그래서 말인데

그래서 말인데 means ***speaking of which***. It is used when one says something that is related to what the other person has just said. This expression is generally used when making a suggestion or a request.

ex A: 부장님, 요즘 영민 씨가 건강이 안 좋은 것 같습니다.
B: 그래서 말인데 영민 씨가 맡고 있는 프로젝트를 마이클 씨가 좀 도와야겠어요.

Script

(1)	Lee Sujeong	Hey, Yeongmin, did you hear the news? Our company performed well this year, so we may get a large bonus this coming Chuseok holidays.
	Park Yeongmin	Really? I hope we do get a big bonus, so that I can give my parents some spending money.
	Lee Sujeong	You're telling me! Our salary is so low that I've never been able to give my parents much spending money. It would be good if we got a large bonus and a pay rise as well.
(2)	Lee Sujeong	Jason, when are you finishing off work? Let's leave together a bit later.
	Jason	I'm sorry, but I'm afraid that I have to go right now. I have a swimming class today.
	Lee Sujeong	Are you taking swimming lessons these days?
	Jason	Yes, I am. I started lessons last month.
	Lee Sujeong	Did you? I'd like to exercise too, but it's hard to find time. I wish they'd make an in-house fitness center so that we can work out at lunch time.
(3)	Jason	Hey, Sujeong. Did you just talk to your daughter on the phone?
	Lee Sujeong	Yes, I did. She calls me so often that sometimes I can't concentrate on my work.
	Jason	She probably wants you to come home.
	Lee Sujeong	You're right. She asks me several times a day when I'm coming home.
	Jason	She's at that age when she needs you a lot.
	Lee Sujeong	Yes. Speaking of which, I wish our company had a day-care center. Then I could see my daughter briefly during the day.
	Jason	Yeah, that would be ideal.
	Lee Sujeong	A lot of Korean companies have in-house day care centers. I hope our company will also make one soon.

Answers

(1) ④ The man hopes that he gets a big bonus this Chuseok holidays, so that he can give his parents more spending money.

(2) ④ The woman wants to work out but it is hard for her to find time. So she hopes that the company will provide an in-house fitness center so that she can exercise at lunch time.

(3) ④ The woman can't see her daughter while at work because her company does not have a day-care center at the workplace.

Vocabulary & Expression

다름이 아니라

다름이 아니라 means ***for no other reason than, for nothing but, just.*** It indicates that there is no other reason than what is stated in the following clause. It is often used when one wants to make a request or ask for a favor. The expression comes directly before what one really wants to say. The expression 다른 게 아니라 is interchangeable with 다름이 아니라.

ex A: 교수님, 드릴 말씀이 있습니다. 다름이 아니라 수업에 대해서 여쭙고 싶은 게 있는데 혹시 오늘 찾아봬도 될까요?
B: 그래요. 오늘 오후 3시에 내 연구실로 오세요.

경솔하게 생각하다

경솔하게 생각하다 means ***to take something too lightly.*** It indicates that one regards something in an overly simple and easy way.

ex A: 너무 힘들어. 내일 당장 사표를 써야겠어.
B: 그렇게 쉽게 결정하면 어떻게 해? 경솔하게 생각하지 말고 조금만 더 차분하게 생각을 해 봐.

Dialogue

Jason	Boss, I have something to ask you.
Boss	What is it?
Jason	I was just wondering if I could have some time off. I have to go home to attend my younger brother's/sister's wedding.
Jason	I hope to get away for a week, beginning next Friday.
Boss	Next Friday? But, our company's workshop is scheduled for that day. Why do you want to take time off that day of all days?
Jason	I was intending to go on the weekend, after the workshop. But I couldn't get a ticket because so many people are going abroad on vacation. I know that it's a big day for our company, and I'm really sorry that I have to go away on that day.
Boss	What about the presentation that you were going to make?
Jason	I'll finish preparing the materials before I leave. I'm thinking of asking Kim Min-su to make the presentation for me.
Boss	Changing the speaker isn't that simple.
Jason	I'm so sorry. I didn't think it over properly.
Boss	I'll speak to the general manager about the speaker. Anyway, I hope you enjoy your younger brother's/sister's wedding.

 p.104

Grammar Focus

-(으)ㄴ/는 데다가 indicates that a certain state or situation becomes more serious because of another added state or situation. When attached to an adjective it takes the form -(으)ㄴ 데다가. When attached to a verb it becomes -는 데다가 and indicates that another state or situation has been added to the present state or situation. When the state or situation referred to is in the past tense, -(으)ㄴ 데다가 is used.

Basic form	-(으)ㄴ 데다가
싸다	싼 데다가
많다	많은 데다가
빨갛다	빨간 데다가

Basic form	-(으)ㄴ 데다가	-는 데다가
주다	준 데다가	주는 데다가
입다	입은 데다가	입는 데다가
만들다	만든 데다가	만드는 데다가

ex A: 이번에 소개시켜 준다는 사람은 어떤 사람이야?
B: 얼굴도 예쁜 데다가 성격도 좋대.

ex A: 우리 학교 학생 식당 어때요?
B: 아주 좋아요. 음식 가격도 싼 데다가 메뉴도 아주 다양해요.

ex A: 다음 달에 학교 근처로 이사한다면서요?
B: 네. 학교 근처에는 편의 시설이 많은 데다가 친구들도 많이 살아서 좋을 것 같아서요.

ex A: 비빔밥이 요즘 외국에서도 인기가 많다면서요?
B: 네. 여러 가지 채소가 많이 들어 있어서 건강에 좋은 데다가 맛도 좋아서 건강 식품으로 인기가 많대요.

ex A: 요즘 몸이 건강해 보여요. 운동하세요?
B: 네. 매일 수영을 하는 데다가 주말에는 테니스도 치니까 몸도 건강해지고 기분도 좋아지는 것 같아요.

ex A: 내일 등산하러 가지 않을래요?
B: 미안해요. 다음에 같이 가요. 내일 오전에는 부모님이 서울에 오시는 데다가 저녁에는 모임도 있거든요.

ex A: 어제 생일 파티 재미있었어요?
B: 네. 선물도 많이 받은 데다가 오랫동안 못 봤던 친구들도 만나서 정말 좋았어요.

ex A: 김영민 씨, 어제까지 제출하기로 한 보고서 아직도 안 됐나요?
B: 죄송합니다. 부장님, 지난주에 출장을 다녀온 데다가 이번 주에는 워크숍 준비하느라 바빠서 아직 못 했습니다.

Focus Plus

- When using -(으)ㄴ/는 데다가, the subject of the preceding clause has to be in agreement with that of the following clause.

  ex 마이클 씨는 잘생긴 데다가 친절하다. (○)
  마이클 씨는 잘생긴 데다가 영민 씨는 친절하다. (×)

- When using -(으)ㄴ/는 데다가, the content of the preceding clause has to be consistent with the content of the following clause. In other words, if the preceding clause is positive, the following clause also has to be positive, and if the preceding clause is negative the following clause also has to be negative.

  ex 하오밍 씨는 공부를 잘하는 데다가 운동도 잘한다. (○)
  하오밍 씨는 공부를 잘하는 데다가 운동을 못한다. (×)

- To indicate that another state or situation has been added to the aforementioned content, the adverbial form 그런 데다가 or 게다가 can be used.

  ex A: 미셸 씨, 오늘 무척 피곤해 보여요.
  B: 감기에 걸려서 몸이 계속 안 좋아요. 게다가 어제 잠도 거의 못 잤고요.

  ex A: 요즘 회사 생활은 좀 어때요?
  B: 요즘 새로운 업무를 맡아서 너무 바빠요. 그런데다가 같이 일하던 동료가 갑자기 회사를 그만두는 바람에 그 일까지 하고 있어요.

- When attached to a noun, the expression becomes N에다가 or N인 데다가. N인 데다가 indicates another thing is added to the noun. N인 데다가 is a contraction of N이다. 게다가, which means another thing is added to the state expressed by the noun.

  ex A: 저녁은 많이 먹었어?
  B: 응. 불고기에다가 냉면까지 먹어서 너무 배불러.

  ex A: 안나 씨, 오늘 무슨 특별한 날이에요? 왜 이렇게 예쁘게 하고 왔어요?
  B: 오늘이 남자 친구 생일인 데다가 만난 지 100일이 되는 날이거든요.

Answers

① A: 왜 술을 안 마셔요?
B: 운전을 해야 하는 데다가 술을 조금만 마셔도 잘 취해서요.

② A: 왜 점심 식사를 안 해요?
B: 제안서를 3시까지 제출해야 하는 데다가 배도 별로 안 고파서요.

③ A: 왜 마케팅 부서에 지원했어요?
B: 전공을 살릴 수 있는 데다가 실무 경험을 하고 싶어서요.

④ A: 왜 아직 퇴근을 못 했어요?
B: 오늘까지 끝내야 할 일이 있는 데다가 이따가 회사 근처에서 약속이 있어서요.

⑤ A: 왜 어제 회식에 안 왔어요?
B: 몸살이 난 데다가 집에 일도 있었어요.

Grammar Focus

–다 보니까 shows that one has come to learn a new fact in the process of performing some action repetitively or persistently, or that there has been a change in state. It is attached to a verb. The expression is interchangeable with –다 보니, –다가 보니, or –다가 보니까.

Basic form	–다 보니까	Basic form	–다 보니까
만나다	만나다 보니까	운동하다	운동하다 보니까
먹다	먹다 보니까	듣다	듣다 보니까
입다	입다 보니까	살다	살다 보니까

ex A: 이번 달에 카드 값이 많이 나왔네요.
B: 이사하느라 이것저것 사다 보니까 이렇게 많이 나왔어요.

ex A: 안나 씨, 한 달 사이에 어떻게 이렇게 날씬해졌어요?
B: 매일 운동을 하다 보니까 저도 모르게 살이 빠졌어요.

ex A: 지난번에 소개받은 사람하고는 어떻게 됐어요?
B: 처음에는 별로였는데 계속 만나다가 보니까 괜찮은 사람인 것 같아서 조금 더 만나 보려고 해요.

ex A: 한국어 쓰기 실력이 많이 좋아졌어요. 어떻게 공부했어요?
B: 한국 친구와 자주 이메일을 주고받다 보니까 이제는 쓰기가 예전만큼 어렵지 않아요.

ex A: 한국 라디오 프로그램을 자주 듣는다면서요? 화면 없이 소리만 들으면 어렵지 않아요?
B: 처음엔 어려웠는데 자주 듣다 보니 생각만큼 어렵지 않아요. 유키 씨도 한번 들어 보세요.

ex A: 미셸 씨는 어쩌면 그렇게 김치를 잘 먹어요?
B: 처음엔 잘 못 먹었는데 한국에서 오래 살다 보니 이젠 김치 없인 밥을 못 먹을 정도예요.

Focus Plus

- When –다 보니까 is attached to an adjective or N이다, it shows that the condition of the preceding clause is the cause of the content of the following clause.

  ex A: 오늘은 평소보다 많이 드시네요. 많이 배고프셨나 봐요.
  B: 배는 별로 안 고팠는데 음식들이 맛있다 보니까 계속 먹게 되네요.

Answers

① 푹신한 침대에서 자다 보니까 딱딱한 바닥에서는 자기 힘들어졌어요.
② 인터넷 전화를 사용하다 보니까 전화 요금 걱정이 없어졌어요.
③ 아침에 일어나자마자 물을 마시다 보니까 변비가 없어졌어요.
④ 그 사람에게 별로 관심이 없었는데 자주 만나다 보니까 점점 정이 들었어요.
⑤ 외국에서 혼자 살다 보니까 음식 솜씨가 많이 늘었어요.

 p.106

Vocabulary & Expression

취업난이 심하다

취업난이 심하다 means that ***employment opportunities are scarce***. This indicates that people find it difficult to get a job because people looking for work outnumber the jobs available. It can be used interchangeably with 취업난이 심각하다. When –난, meaning "crisis," is added to the end of a noun, it denotes difficulty or scarcity in relation to that noun. For example, 주택난 signifies a housing shortage, and 인력난 represents a shortage of available workers in the job market.

ex A: 요즘 자기 전공 공부보다 외국어 공부를 더 열심히 하는 대학생이 많은 것 같아요.
B: 취업난이 심해서 그럴 거예요. 좋은 회사에 취직하려면 외국어를 잘하는 게 중요하거든요.

Script

Kim Sujin	Are you satisfied with the company you're working for?
Park Yeongmin	Why? What makes you ask such a question?
Kim Sujin	A newspaper article says that one out of three office workers are dissatisfied with their jobs.
Park Yeongmin	Really? Most people tend to find something they're not happy about as they work.
Kim Sujin	According to the article, the largest number of respondents expressed dissatisfaction with the heavy workload. You also always seem to be busy. Do you really have a lot to handle at work?
Park Yeongmin	Yes, I have so much work that I often have to work on the weekends. I have a lot to do outside the office and frequently go on business trips outside of Seoul.
Kim Sujin	Oh, I see. I just wished I could get a job, but I guess working in an office has its own difficulties.
Park Yeongmin	Yeah. Work is not easy. When I graduated from college, unemployment was serious, so I thought I would be happy if I could just get employed. But after working for several years, I wonder if I'm really suited to my job. I had a change of heart. Besides, the company I'm working for pays a really low salary.
Kim Sujin	Even so, I envy you because you have a job.
Park Yeongmin	Don't worry, you'll soon find a job. I hope you get to work somewhere that you really want to.

Answers

(1) ② The major reason for the majority of office workers' dissatisfaction with their jobs is the heavy workload.

(2) ② The man's dissatisfaction comes from the thought that he is not suited to the job and the low salary.

Vocabulary & Expression

생각이 굴뚝같다

생각이 굴뚝같다 means that ***one wants something badly***. It indicates that one wants something or some situation to happen very much.

ex A: 내일이라도 당장 배낭 하나 메고 떠나고 싶은 생각이 굴뚝같아요.
B: 저도 회사일로 스트레스를 받을 때마다 어디론가 떠나고 싶다는 생각을 자주 해요.

월급이 쥐꼬리만 하다

월급이 쥐꼬리만 하다 means that ***one's salary as small as a mouse's tail***. So to speak, it indicates one has a very small salary.

ex A: 이번 달부터 세금이 또 오른대요.
B: 또요? 쥐꼬리만 한 월급 받아서 세금까지 내고 나면 남는 게 없는데 걱정이네요.

Dialogue

Jason	Yeongmin, I have something on my mind these days. Do you have time to talk?
Park Yeongmin	Sure, go ahead.
Jason	I'm worried about my work.
Park Yeongmin	What's bothering you? Tell me more about it.
Jason	Actually, I think about quitting so many times everyday.
Park Yeongmin	Really? I didn't notice that you were having such a hard time, even though I'm right next to you. Why do you want to quit?
Jason	I've performed poorly in all the projects that I've been given and I'm worn out. In addition, I'm not suited to the work at all. On top of that, relationships with people at work are difficult too.
Park Yeongmin	I didn't know you were so troubled. I've had lots of hard times too because of work and other people.
Jason	In addition, holidays are short and the pay is so low.
Park Yeongmin	No office workers think they're well paid.
Jason	I know. But I wish I could get a raise and rest properly on weekends. More than anything else, I really want to enjoy my work.
Park Yeongmin	Yes, me too. Just hang in there, OK? You've done well so far. The holidays will arrive soon, and we'll be getting a bonus.
Jason	You're right. That would be the best thing to do. Thanks for listening to me. I know you're busy because you have so much work to do.

Vocabulary & Expression

발 디딜 틈이 없다

발 디딜 틈이 없다 literally means ***to have no place to put down one's feet***. This is used to describe a place or event that is very crowded.

ex A: 어제 벚꽃 축제에 잘 다녀왔어요? 사진은 많이 찍었어요.
B: 사람이 발 디딜 틈 없이 많아서 사진은 거의 못 찍었어요.

생각이 스치다

생각이 스치다 means ***to have a thought flit through one's mind***. It indicates that a thought came to one's head briefly and then disappeared.

ex A: 창밖의 눈 오는 모습이 정말 아름답다. 그렇지?
B: 응. 눈 오는 모습을 보니까 여러 가지 생각이 스치고 지나가네. 고향 생각도 나고.

배꼽시계가 울리다

배꼽시계가 울리다 literally means ***one's belly clock is ringing***. This is a metaphorical expression that likens the state of being hungry to an alarm clock ringing in one's stomach.

ex A: 벌써 점심시간인가 봐요. 제 배꼽시계가 울리는데요.
B: 저도 배 속이 꼬르륵거리기 시작했어요. 빨리 점심 먹으러 갑시다.

졸음이 쏟아지다

졸음이 쏟아지다 means ***to be very sleepy***. It indicates a state of extreme sleepiness. 졸음이 쏟아지다 is used interchangeably with 졸음이 몰려오다. To express the attempt to chase sleep away, the expression 졸음을 쫓다 can be used.

ex 운전 중 졸음이 쏟아질 때는 졸음을 참기보다 차를 세우고 잠깐 수면을 취하는 것이 좋다.

Reading Guide

This passage is about office worker Kim's daily routine, from waking in the morning, going to work, at work, to leaving the office at the end of the day. Read the passage carefully, thinking what he is doing, when, and in what order. (☞『이화 한국어 3-2』 p.110)

Answers

(1) ④ When Kim arrives at the office, he first checks his email, looks up news, and then starts work.
(2) 12시가 되면 항상 배가 고프다.

–쟁이

p.113

Vocabulary Expansion

When the suffix –쟁이 is attached to a noun, it indicates a person with the traits or properties of that noun. The term –쟁이 is often used to address such a person disparagingly.

월급쟁이
salaried worker

This is a derogative term for a salaried employee.

ex A: 우리 회사에서는 구내식당이 있어서 점심값을 아낄 수 있어서 좋은 것 같아요.
B: 맞아요. 우리 같은 월급쟁이한테는 점심값이라도 아낄 수 있다는 게 중요하지요.

욕심쟁이
greedy person

This term refers to a greedy person. It can be used interchangeably with 욕심꾸러기.

ex A: 우리 아이는 욕심쟁이여서 뭐든지 양보할 줄을 몰라서 걱정이에요.
B: 아직 나이가 어려서 그럴 거예요. 조금 크면 달라지겠죠.

점쟁이
fortune-teller

This is a derogative term for a person who makes a living by predicting the future for other people.

ex A: 어제 점쟁이한테 가서 남자 친구하고 언제 결혼하는 게 좋은지 물어봤는데 늦게 결혼하라고 하더라고요.
B: 그런 말 믿지 마세요. 자기 인생은 자기 스스로 결정하는 거죠.

거짓말쟁이
liar

This term refers to a person who repeatedly tells lies.

ex A: 마이클 씨가 하는 말은 믿지 마세요. 거짓말을 정말 많이 해요.
B: 그래요? 저는 마이클 씨가 거짓말쟁이인지 몰랐어요.

수다쟁이
chatterbox

This term refers to a person who is unnecessarily talkative.

ex A: 예전과 달리 요즘에는 여자보다 더 말이 많은 남자들이 많은 것 같아요.
B: 맞아요. 요즘은 여자들보다 남자들이 더 수다쟁이인 것 같아요.

고집쟁이
bullhead

This term is used to address a person who sticks to his/her ideas doggedly.

ex A: 내 동생은 고집쟁이라서 한번 자기가 하고 싶은 게 있으면 옆에서 아무리 말해도 듣지 않아.
B: 고집이 센 게 장점이 될 때도 있어. 자기 생각이 분명하잖아.

겁쟁이
coward

This term refers to a person who is not brave and fears many things.

ex A: 마이클 씨, 길에서 강도를 잡았다면서요? 무섭지 않았어요?
B: 조금 무섭기는 했지만 겁쟁이처럼 모르는 척할 순 없었어요.

허풍쟁이
big talker

This term refers to a person with a penchant for exaggerating or overacting.

ex A: 영민 씨가 배우 이현민하고 제일 친한 친구라면서요?
B: 아니요. 그냥 고등학교 동창일 뿐이에요. 아무튼 영민 씨는 허풍쟁이예요.

Vocabulary Check

Part 1 준비합시다 01

- 입사하다 to join a company
- 승진하다 to be promoted
- 회계사 accountant
- 비우다 to vacate, to empty
- 발표자 speaker
- 상의하다 to consult, to discuss
- 진료 medical treatment
- 신입 사원 new recruit

Part 1 준비합시다 02

- 잦다 to be frequent
- 새벽같이 at daybreak
- 상대하다 to deal with
- 고객 client, customer
- 까다롭다 to be fussy, to be fastidious
- 도로 road
- 시차 jet lag
- 적응하다 to adapt oneself to
- 드물다 to be rare, to be unusual

Part 1 들어 봅시다

- 상여금 bonus
- 인상 raise, rise, increase
- 사내 at work
- 보육 childcare, day care
- 개발비 development expense
- 지원 support
- 근무 work

Part 1 말해 봅시다

- 대책 measure
- 부하 subordinate
- 제기하다 to raise, to bring up
- 경솔하다 to be careless
- 상사 boss, superior
- 용건 a matter to attend to
- 조퇴 leaving early
- 무책임하다 to be irresponsible
- 맡다 to assume, to undertake

Part 2 준비합시다 01

- 구내식당 office cafeteria
- 불경기 recession, economic slump
- 취업난 high unemployment
- 안정적 stable, secure
- 기업 enterprise, company
- 이미지 impression, reputation
- 제안서 proposal, memorandum
- 마케팅 marketing
- 부서 department, division
- 살리다 to make use of
- 실무 work, business

Part 2 준비합시다 02

- 시청하다 to watch (TV)
- 푹신하다 to be soft

Part 2 들어 봅시다

- 대인 관계 interpersonal relationships

Part 2 말해 봅시다

- 지경 to be in a situation
- 쥐꼬리만 하다 to be as small as a mouse's tail

Part 3 읽어 봅시다

- 미혼 unmarried, single
- 냉수 cold water
- 외치다 to cry out, to shout out

- 건네주다 to hand over, to deliver
- 싣다 to load, to take in
- 디디다 to take a step
- 틈 room, space
- 활기차다 to be energetic
- 스치다 to flash past
- 열중하다 to be absorbed in
- 배꼽시계 belly clock
- 취침 to go to bed/sleep

Part 3 어휘를 늘려 봅시다

- 단짝 best friend

Topic Vocabulary

Work

- 취직 시험을 보다 to take an employment exam
- 면접을 보다 to have a job interview
- 취직이 되다 to get a job
- 퇴사하다 to quit a job
- 조퇴하다 to leave work early
- 결근하다 to be absent from work, to stay home from work
- 야근하다 to work overtime, to work at night
- 휴가를 내다 to take time off
- 휴직을 하다 to take a leave of absence
- 월급을 받다 to receive monthly pay, to get a salary
- 상여금을 받다 to receive a bonus
- 수당을 받다 to receive an allowance (benefits)
- 신입 사원 new employee/recruit
- 경력 사원 experienced employee
- 직장 상사 one's boss/superior
- 부하 직원 junior staff
- 월급이 오르다 to get a pay raise
- 월급이 인상되다 to get a pay raise
- 월급이 깎이다 to get a pay cut
- 경력직으로 취직하다 to join a company as an experienced employee
- 외근하다 to work outside the office
- 해외 출장을 가다 to go on an overseas business trip
- 회식을 하다 to have a staff/work dinner
- 연수를 받다 to attend a training session
- 회사를 그만두다 to quit one's job
- 퇴직금을 받다 to receive severance pay
- 정년퇴직을 하다 to retire at the regular retirement age

 p.118

Grammar Focus

–(으)려던 참이다 shows that one intends to do something at the moment of speaking or in the near future. In particular, this expression is often used to indicate that one intended or planned to do something related to a suggestion made by the other person. It is attached to a verb. In addition, it is generally used with words such as 마침, 막, 이제, 지금, 그렇지 않아도, and 안 그래도.

Basic form	–(으)려던 참이다	Basic form	–(으)려던 참이다
가다	가려던 참이다	입다	입으려던 참이다
말하다	말하려던 참이다	듣다	들으려던 참이다
먹다	먹으려던 참이다	붓다	부으려던 참이다

ex A: 내일 시험이라 공부해야 하는데 너무 졸려요.
B: 저도 졸려서 커피 사러 나가려던 참인데 영민 씨 것도 사다 드릴까요?

ex A: 여보세요. 아키라 씨, 오랜만이에요. 잘 지내시죠?
B: 아, 민정 씨, 그렇지 않아도 요즘 잘 지내나 궁금해서 전화하려던 참이었어요.

ex A: 오늘 신문이 어디에 있는지 알아? 아무리 찾아도 안 보이네.
B: 여기 있어. 내가 막 읽으려던 참이었는데 너 먼저 읽을래?

ex A: 오늘 비가 내려서 그런지 좀 쌀쌀한데 창문을 닫을까요?
B: 안 그래도 추워서 창문을 닫으려던 참이었는데 제가 닫을게요.

ex A: 저녁에 약속 있다면서 왜 준비 안 해?
B: 안 나가도 돼. 옷을 막 입으려던 참이었는데 친구가 갑자기 일이 생겼다고 약속을 취소했어.

ex A: 배가 출출한데 우리 떡볶이 만들어 먹을까?
B: 그래? 컵라면에 막 물을 부으려던 참이었는데…… 그럼 컵라면 말고 떡볶이 먹지 뭐.

Answers

① A: 놀이공원에 놀러 가려고 하는데 같이 갈래요?
B: 잘됐네요. 안 그래도 시험이 끝나서 놀려던 참이었어요.

② A: 일요일에 등산을 하려고 하는데 같이 갈래요?
B: 마침 잘됐네요. 그렇지 않아도 운동 부족이라서 운동을 하려던 참이었어요.

③ A: 명절에 선생님을 뵈러 가려고 하는데 같이 갈래요?
B: 잘됐네요. 안 그래도 상의할 일이 있어서 찾아뵈려던 참이었어요.

④ A: 책을 빌리러 도서관에 가는데 같이 갈래요?
B: 네. 안 그래도 저도 시험공부 때문에 도서관에 가려던 참이었어요.

⑤ A: 친구 생일 선물을 사러 백화점에 가려고 하는데 같이 갈래요?
B: 잘됐네요. 마침 화장품이 떨어져서 사려던 참이었거든요.

Grammar Focus

-느라고 is used to indicate that a preceding action is ongoing, making one unable to do something else or producing an undesirable outcome. It is often used to make an excuse for a negative result or for a situation where one could not do anything. It is attached to a verb and can be abbreviated to -느라.

Basic form	-느라고	Basic form	-느라고
자다	자느라고	돕도	돕느라고
공부하다	공부하느라고	놀다	노느라고
먹다	먹느라고	팔다	파느라고
듣다	듣느라고	만들다	만드느라고

ex A: 용돈을 받은 지 며칠이나 됐다고 벌써 돈이 떨어졌어?
B: 엄마, 죄송해요. 친구들하고 부산에 가느라고 돈을 많이 썼거든요.

ex A: 요즘 왜 그렇게 동아리 모임에서 얼굴 보기가 힘들어요?
B: 요즘 공부할 것도 많은데 아르바이트까지 하느라 바빠서 동아리에 나가기가 어려워요.

ex A: 주말에 제주도에 갔다 왔다면서요? 사진 많이 찍었어요?
B: 아니요. 친구들 사진을 찍어 주느라고 제 사진은 많이 못 찍었어요.

ex A: 언니, 다음 달이 아버지 환갑이신데 무슨 선물을 하면 좋을까?
B: 그동안 우리들 키우시느라고 여행 한 번 제대로 못 가셨는데 여행을 보내드리면 어떨까?

ex A: 아까 택배 아저씨가 오셨다가 집에 아무도 없어서 그냥 가셨대요.
B: 그래요? 집에 계속 있었는데 음악을 듣느라고 초인종 소리를 못 들었나 봐요.

ex A: 유키야, 집들이에 초대해 줘서 고마워. 혼자서 음식을 만드느라고 많이 힘들었겠다.
B: 아니야. 율리아가 일찍 와서 도와줘서 별로 힘들지 않았어.

ex A: 아까 여러 번 전화했었는데. 왜 전화 안 받았어요?
B: 미안해요. 카페에서 친구들과 수다 떠느라고 전화가 온 줄 몰랐어요.

Focus Plus

- When -느라고 is used, the subject of the preceding clause has to be in agreement with that of the following clause.

  ex 오빠가 여자 친구 선물을 사느라고 (오빠가) 돈을 다 썼다. (○)

  ex 오빠가 여자 친구 선물을 사느라고 엄마가 돈을 다 썼다. (×)

- In the clause following -느라고, the imperative or propositive form cannot be used.

  ex 우리 친구를 만나느라고 명동에 갈까요? (×)

  ex 아침에 늦잠을 자느라고 지각하지 마세요. (×)

- When expressing one's gratitude for efforts made by someone else, expressions like -느라(고) 고생하다, -느라(고) 수고하다, or -느라(고) 힘들다 can be used.

ex 늦은 시간까지 일하시느라 힘드셨지요?

ex 먼 길 오시느라 고생이 많으셨어요.

ex 장시간 운전하시느라고 수고하셨습니다.

- -느라고 can also be used when the preceding clause simply serves as the purpose of the following clause. In this case -느라고 is interchangeable with -기 위해서. However, -느라고 often indicates the action undertaken in the preceding clause for the purpose or situation in the following clause is troublesome or involves some sacrifice.

ex A: 아침 일찍 강의를 듣느라고 7시에 집에서 나왔어요.
B: 7시에요? 피곤하겠네요. 그럼 커피 한잔 마시러 가요.

- -느라고 is used to describe a situation where the continuity of the action in the preceding clause affects the following clause. Therefore, it has to be used with a verb that indicates continuity of an action or a verb that depends on the intent of the subject of the sentence. For example, -느라고 cannot be used with a verb that does not require any intent on the part of the subject or that represents a momentary action such as 감기에 걸리다, 기침이 나다, 넘어지다, and 일어나다.

ex 감기에 걸리느라고 학교에 못 갔어요. (×)

ex 늦게 일어나느라고 회사에 늦었어요. (×)

ex 돌에 걸려 넘어지느라고 다리를 다쳤어요. (×)

- -느라고 and -노라고 are often mistakenly used. The expression -노라고 indicates a situation where a certain action undertaken at the one's best efforts produced an unsatisfactory outcome. It is also often used by the speaker to relate his/her own actions with humility.

ex A: 기말 과제를 잘해서 냈어? 오늘까지 제출해야 하잖아?
B: 열심히 하노라고 했는데 별로 잘한 것 같지가 않아. 마지막에 결론 부분을 잘 못 쓴 것 같아.

正解

① B: 미안해요. 보고서를 쓰느라고 정신이 없어서 늦었어요.
대신에 제가 맛있는 거 사 드릴게요. 기분 푸세요.

② B: 미안해요. 아이를 맡기고 오느라 시간이 걸려서 늦었어요.
대신에 제가 커피 사 드릴게요. 기분 푸세요.

③ B: 미안해요. 회의 준비를 하느라고 너무 바빠서 깜박했어요.
대신에 제가 맛있는 저녁 살게요. 기분 푸세요.

④ B: 미안해요. 열쇠를 찾느라 빨리 못 나왔어요. 대신에 제가 저녁 살게요. 기분 푸세요.

⑤ B: 미안해요. 전화로 수다를 떠느라고 시간 가는 줄 몰랐어요.
대신에 제가 맛있는 저녁을 사 줄게요. 기분 푸세요.

Vocabulary & Expression

마음이 흔들리다

마음이 흔들리다 means ***(one's mind) to be moved***. It is used to indicate that the speaker's resolution is shaken or thoughts are disturbed.

ex A: 영민 씨, 이제 정말 담배 끊을 거죠?
B: 네. 그런데 담배 피우는 사람 옆에 가면 담배 냄새 때문에 자꾸 마음이 흔들려요.

Script

(1) Haoming: Mom, I want to talk to you.
Mom: Do you? I've been trying to talk to you as well. Have you decided on your major?
Haoming: Yes, I have. I want to major in music in college.
Mom: Music? You can pursue music as a hobby. I'd like you to study business management, to boost your career opportunities in some way...
Haoming: Mom, I don't want to waste four years studying business management when I'm not interested in it.
Mom: No one is good at everything from the beginning. If you study hard, you'll develop an interest in business management.
Haoming: Mom, I know what you are worrying about. But I can also live a good life by majoring in music. More than anything else, I believe that doing what I really want to do and what I'm good at is the key to success. Mom, why don't you try believing in me?
Mom: Well, right now we think very differently. Why don't we think about it some more and talk again later?

(2) Yuki: Why don't we go to the sea on summer vacation? We can swim and sunbathe.
Park Yeongmin: What do you mean? The seaside is so crowded that it's hard to find a spot to lie down and sunbathe, and if you want to buy something you have to stand in a long queue. It's so exhausting that it's hard to relax. Wouldn't it be better to spend our summer vacation at a pension located in the woods with fresh air rather than at the seaside?
Yuki: That may be so, but it will be expensive to book a pension in the peak summer season.
Park Yeongmin: The room charges have come down a lot these days. And the pension that I picked for this summer vacation has a swimming pool. So we can enjoy swimming as well as sunbathing. In addition, there is a famous film location nearby, which should be fun to visit.
Yuki: A film location? I've been wanting to go there. Shall we do as you say?
Park Yeongmin: Yes. Just trust me. You won't regret it.

Answers

(1) ③ **The son has no interest in business management and does not want to study it in college.**

(2) ① **Upon hearing the man's explanation, the woman changed her mind and decided to spend the summer vacation at the location that he recommended.**

Vocabulary & Expression

같이 도자기 축제에 가면 안 돼?

같이 도자기 축제에 가면 안 돼? means ***Why don't you come to the ceramics festival with me?*** It is used to make the proposal of going to the ceramics festival together. The expression –(으)면 안 돼? is sometimes used to ask whether a certain action is possible or not. However, in colloquial langage, it is often used to make a suggestion or a request.

ex A: 오늘 좀 매운 음식을 먹고 싶은데 우리 점심에 김치찌개 먹으러 가면 안 돼?
B: 그래. 그럼 식당은 네가 정해.

기회를 놓치다

기회를 놓치다 means ***to miss an opportunity/chance***. 기회를 잃다 is a similar expre-ssion. 놓치다 is often used to indicate that something was not done because the right time for doing it passed by. Related expressions include 시기를 놓치다 and 때를 놓치다.

ex A: 부장님이 미국에서 하는 해외 연수 과정에 저를 추천해 주셨는데 갈지 말지 고민이에요.
B: 그렇게 망설이다가 기회를 놓치면 너무 아쉽잖아요. 일단 한번 가 보세요.

Dialogue

Huong	Anna, I'm glad I caught you! I was just about to call you.
Anna	Why? What's up?
Huong	Do you have any plans for this weekend?
Anna	I'm going to the movies with Julian.
Huong	Really? I wanted to go to the ceramics festival with you this weekend... I heard that we could make our own pottery there.
Anna	The ceramics festival? I also wanted to go to that festival, too.
Huong	What about going to the movies next week and going to the ceramics festival with me this weekend instead? You can see a movie next week, can't you?
Anna	Well... I think I'll be busy preparing for the exams next week. Even though the exams are coming up, I haven't been able to find time to study because of my part-time job. I'm afraid I'll have to give up the ceramics festival this weekend.
Huong	I understand, but the festival is held only once a year. If you miss the chance, you'll regret it. Please think it over again.
Anna	Yeah, you're right. But Julian might be disappointed.
Huong	Well, why don't we ask him to join us? He won't regret it, either. Trust me.
Anna	Okay. I'll talk to Julian about it.

Grammar Focus

-(으)ㄹ 수밖에 없다 means "cannot help ~ing." It indicates that a certain situation is inevitable because there are no other possibilities or options. When attached to an adjective, the expression suggests that it is natural for such an outcome to follow. When attached to a verb, it indicates that there is no choice but to take such an action.

Basic form	-(으)ㄹ 수밖에 없다	Basic form	-(으)ㄹ 수밖에 없다
크다	클 수밖에 없다	가다	갈 수밖에 없다
많다	많을 수밖에 없다	먹다	먹을 수밖에 없다
무겁다	무거울 수밖에 없다	걷다	걸을 수밖에 없다

ex A: 오늘 몸이 너무 아파서 학교에 못 갈 것 같아요.
B: 평소에 안 하던 운동을 갑자기 5시간이나 했으니 몸이 아플 수밖에 없지.

ex A: 마이클 씨는 어떻게 그렇게 친구가 많을까요?
B: 누구에게나 친절하고 성격이 좋으니까 친구가 많을 수밖에 없지요.

ex A: 오늘 너무 덥지 않아?
B: 난 딱 좋은데. 너는 그렇게 두꺼운 옷을 입었으니까 더울 수밖에 없지.

ex A: 내가 저번에 비밀이라고 했는데 그걸 왜 다른 사람들한테 말했어?
B: 미안해. 사람들이 자꾸 물어봐서 말할 수밖에 없었어.

ex A: 여기는 버스가 안 다니는 길이야. 택시 잡기도 조금 힘들고.
B: 그래? 그럼 걸어서 갈 수 밖에 없겠다. 조금 힘들지만 걸어가자.

ex A: 이사 가고 싶다고 했었지요? 집은 구했어요?
B: 아니요. 마땅한 집을 못 찾아서 여기서 계속 살 수밖에 없을 것 같아요.

Answers

① A: 주말에 영화 잘 봤어요?
B: 아니요. 표가 매진돼서 그냥 집으로 돌아올 수밖에 없었어요.

② A: 친구하고 수영 잘했어요?
B: 아니요. 갑자기 감기에 걸려서 약속을 취소할 수밖에 없었어요.

③ A: 이사할 집을 알아봤어요?
B: 아니요. 급한 일이 생기는 바람에 못 알아봤어요. 그래서 다음 주에 알아볼 수밖에 없을 것 같아요.

④ A: 저번에 새로 산 원피스를 어제 입었어요?
B: 아니요. 살이 쪄서 다른 옷을 입을 수밖에 없었어요.

⑤ A: 어제 집에서 한국 음식을 만들어 먹었어요?
B: 아니요. 음식을 만들다가 태워서 라면을 먹을 수밖에 없었어요.

Grammar Focus

-(으)ㄴ/는 김에 is used to indicate that when a certain action is taken or a certain event has already taken place, another unplanned action related to the previous one will be performed. It is attached to a verb and often comes with adverbial phrases such as 기왕(에), 이왕(에), or 어차피.

Basic form	-는 김에	-(으)ㄴ 김에
가다	가는 김에	간 김에
먹다	먹는 김에	먹은 김에
만들다	만드는 김에	만든 김에
묻다	묻는 김에	물은 김에
팔다	파는 김에	판 김에
짓다	짓는 김에	지은 김에

ex A: 저 지금 슈퍼마켓에 갈 건데 뭐 부탁할 거 있어요?
B: 마침 잘됐네요. 그럼 슈퍼마켓에 가는 김에 음료수랑 과자 좀 사다 줄래요?

ex A: 오늘 점심은 어느 식당에 가서 먹을까요?
B: 오늘은 사무실에서 먹어요. 제 도시락을 싸는 김에 안나 씨 도시락도 싸 왔어요.

ex A: 룸메이트가 방을 너무 더럽게 써서 더 이상 못 참겠어. 당장 룸메이트 바꿔 달라고 해야겠어.
B: 방학이 다음 주인데 이왕 참는 김에 조금만 더 참아.

ex A: 오늘 무슨 날이에요? 웬 음식을 이렇게 많이 만들었어요?
B: 오늘따라 고향 음식이 생각나서요. 기왕 고향 음식을 만드는 김에 먹고 싶은 음식을 다 만들어 봤어요.

ex A: 요코 씨, 정말 오랜만이에요. 그동안 어떻게 지냈어요?
B: 일이 많았어요. 그러지 말고 오랜만에 만난 김에 식사나 하러 갈까요? 할 이야기가 많아요.

ex A: 지금 나가면 저녁 모임에 늦는 거 아니야?
B: 맞아. 그런데 어차피 늦은 김에 천천히 가려고.

Focus Plus

- -는 김에 is used to indicate an unplanned action taken in relation to another action. On the other hand, -는 길에 (See 『이화 한국어 2-2』 Chapter 10, p.63) indicates an action taken on the way to or on the occasion of going to or coming from a certain place. -는 김에 is used with various verbs, whereas -는 길에 is used only with verbs indicating movement such as 가다 and 오다.

ex A: 저 지금 서점에 갈 건데 부탁할 거 있어요?
B: 저도 살 책이 있었는데 잘됐네요. 그럼 미안하지만 서점에 가는 김에 제 책도 사다 주시겠어요?

ex A: 왜 이렇게 늦었어요?
B: 미안해요. 여기 오는 길에 우연히 친구를 만났거든요.

- –는 김에 is used when a certain action is followed by another unplanned action that is related to the former. –(으)ㄴ/는 김에 is used to indicate that when a certain action is taken or a certain event has already taken place, another unplanned action related to the previous one will be performed.

  ex A: 다음 주에 부산에 출장 가는데 하루 이틀 더 머물면서 좀 쉬다 오려고요.
  B: 그럼 기왕 부산에 가는 김에 회도 좀 먹고 바다도 보고 오세요.

  ex A: 학교 도서관에 책 반납하러 가는데 같이 갈래?
  B: 오후에 약속이 있어서 못 갈 것 같아. 미안한데 네 것 반납하는 김에 내 책도 좀 반납해 주면 안 될까?

  ex A: 부산에 온 김에 회 먹을까요?
  B: 좋아요. 안 그래도 저녁에 회를 먹자고 말하려던 참이었어요.

  ex A: 이치로 씨가 다음 달에 귀국한다는데 우리 송별회를 해야 하지 않을까?
  B: 그래. 그럼 말이 나온 김에 송별회 계획을 짜 보자.

- 화가 난 김에 can be replaced by the single-word expression 홧김에. The expressions 길을 나선 김에 and 시작된 김에 can be substituted by the single-word expression 내친김에.

  ex A: 남자 친구하고 아직도 화해를 안 했어?
  B: 응. 내가 홧김에 헤어지자고 했더니 그냥 가버리더라고. 그 이후로 서로 연락도 안 하고 있어.

  ex A: 왜 이렇게 늦게 들어왔어?
  B: 친구 만나러 시내에 갔다가 내친김에 쇼핑도 좀 하느라고 좀 늦었어.

Answers

① A: 저 지금 방을 치우려고 하는데 뭐 부탁할 거 있어요?
B: 잘됐네요. 그럼 방을 치우는 김에 쓰레기통을 비워 주세요.

② A: 지금 케이크를 만들려고 하는데 뭐 먹고 싶은 거 있어요?
B: 잘됐네요. 케이크를 만드는 김에 과자도 만들어 주세요.

③ A: 저 지금 유키를 만나려고 하는데 뭐 부탁할 거 있어요?
B: 잘됐네요. 유키를 만나는 김에 제가 유키에게 빌린 CD도 좀 전해 주세요.

④ A: 출출해서 라면을 끓이려고 하는데 제니 씨는 뭐 안 드실래요?
B: 저도 마침 출출했는데. 라면을 끓이는 김에 한 개 더 끓여 주세요.

⑤ A: 쇼핑하러 백화점에 가려고 하는데 뭐 부탁할 거 있어요?
B: 백화점에 가는 김에 빵집에 들러서 빵을 좀 사다 주세요.

Vocabulary & Expression

부쩍 늘다

부쩍 늘다 means (something) ***to suddenly increase.*** This is used to express that the state, frequency, or amount of a thing or a condition has suddenly increased. 부쩍 is an adverb used to stress that something has suddenly risen or fallen.

ex A: 학생 식당에서 밥을 먹는 학생들이 요즘 들어 부쩍 늘어난 것 같아요.
B: 식당의 메뉴가 요즘 다양해져서 그런 것 같아요.

Script

Host: It is said there is a sudden increase these days in the number of people who are distressed by human relationships. One of the most important and difficult things to handle in social life is perhaps interpersonal relations. So today the renowned sociologist Kim Yuna will discuss ways to form harmonious human relationships. Let's hear a round of applause for today's speaker.

Speaker: Hello, everyone. (To the host) Your dress today is lovely.

Host: Thank you! You look beautiful today, too.

Speaker: Thank you! Well, folks, your TV host and I met for the first time today, but we observe each other very closely. Why? The key is praise. Even a small compliment makes us very happy. Compliments can also make relationships smoother. But we're not used to giving compliments to each other, so we're not very generous with praise. There is, however, nothing like words of praise to make people happy and move them. Remember, saying good things about others is a habit. Try to see other people's good points and compliment them and make them smile. In this way, you can build a good relationship with each other. Now that I've mentioned it, why don't you try complimenting the person seated next to you?
(Audience members praise the person sitting beside them)

Host: As you say, praising each other seems to make the mood brighter. (To the speaker) But, I'm also sparing with praise. It's not because I'm not used to giving compliments, but rather because complimentary remarks can be interpreted as false flattery. Is there a good way to make a natural, pleasant complimentary remark?

Answers

(1) ② The host began by mentioning that recently more and more people are concerned about interpersonal relationships.

(2) ② Although the host and the speaker are meeting each other for the first time, they seem to be on good terms owing to the compliments they have exchanged.

(3) ② At the end of the lecture, the host asked the speaker about ways to praise others in a natural and pleasant manner.

Vocabulary & Expression

말도 마세요

말도 마세요 means ***don't even talk about it, you don't know the half of it***. This is used to indicate that something is so great or severe that there is no need to talk about it further. This expression can be used in both a positive and negative sense. When used with friends or someone younger or lower in position, 말도 마 is used.

ex A: 이번 시험은 어땠어? 잘 봤어?
B: 말도 마. 1번부터 너무 어려워서 끝까지 다 풀지도 못했어.

도저히 안 될 것 같다

도저히 안 될 것 같다 means ***it seems impossible***. The word 도저히 means no "matter what is done," and is usually used in a negative sentence.

ex A: 내일까지 이 보고서를 다 끝낼 수 있겠어요?
B: 정리할 자료가 많아서 내일까지는 도저히 안 될 것 같아요.

Dialogue

Jason	Hey, Yeongmin, you look very busy. Is something wrong?
Park Yeongmin	You don't know the half of it. On Wednesday afternoon, I have an important contract to sign and on the same day I have a visitor from a client company in the U.S. So I'm really busy with preparations and don't even have time for lunch.
Jason	Sounds tough. Even so, you need to eat. I'm a bit hungry and am going to the shop on the 1st floor. Can I get you something?
Park Yeongmin	Thanks, Jason. While you're there, could you get me a sandwich?
Jason	Sure. No problem.
Park Yeongmin	Thank you!
Jason	Don't mention it. Is there anything else?
Park Yeongmin	I'm a bit hesitant to ask... But could you pick up the visitor at the airport on Wednesday afternoon?
Jason	Oh... I'm sorry, I don't think I can make it.
Park Yeongmin	Really? Can't you help me, please? An important deal has to be signed that day, so I have to work outside the office.
Jason	Oh, I'm sorry. I'd help you if I could. But I have a business trip to Busan that day, so I don't think I can do it. Sorry.
Park Yeongmin	That's alright. I'm sorry for troubling you.

Vocabulary & Expression

무심코 한 말

무심코 한 말 means ***words uttered inadvertently***. 무심코 is often used to express a situation where a certain action is taken without thinking or without any particular intention.

ex A: 아이들에게 항상 말조심을 해야 해요. 어른들이 무심코 한 말 한마디에도 아이들은 상처를 받을 수 있어요.
B: 저도 그래서 요즘 아이들 앞에서 항상 말조심 하고 있어요.

상처를 입다

상처를 입다 means ***to get hurt***. Expressions such as 상처를 받다 and 상처가 나다 are synonymous with 상처를 입다. On the contrary, expressions such as 상처를 주다, 상처를 입히다, or 상처를 남기다 are used to indicate hurting or inflicting wounds on another person.

ex A: 부부가 서로에게 가장 상처를 주는 말이 어떤 걸까요?
B: 다른 사람과 비교하는 말인 것 같아요. 주변의 다른 사람과 비교하는 말을 들으면 누구든지 마음에 상처를 입어요.

이와는 달리

이와는 달리 means ***on the contrary***. It is a literary expression used to indicate that the information in the following sentence is opposed to the information in the preceding one when compared with each other. 이와는 달리 can be replaced by expressions like 반면(에), 한편, or 이와는 대조적으로.

ex 대부분의 한국 대학은 3월에 새로운 학기가 시작된다.
이와는 달리 미국 대학은 일반적으로 9월에 새로운 학기가 시작된다.

Reading Guide

This passage shows the various types of responses given by people when they are displeased at a causal remark made by someone else. Read it carefully, thinking which type you belong to. (☞「이화 한국어 3-2」 p.130)

Answers

(1) ④ The passage is about the variety of responses shown by people when they hear something offensive.

(2) ② The passage stresses that before speaking, you should remember it is important not to hurt another person's feelings or pride.

얼굴 관련 표현

p.133

Vocabulary Expansion

얼굴을 내밀다
to make an appearance

This means to attend a gathering of many people.

ex A: 내일 동아리 모임에 갈 거야?
B: 응, 그런데 오후에 중요한 약속이 있어서 잠깐 얼굴만 내밀고 가야 할 것 같아.

얼굴을 들다
to hold one's head high

This indicates one deals with other people with confidence and without shame.

ex A: 엄마, 언니가 내가 취직 시험에 떨어진 걸 여기저기 말하고 다니는 바람에 얼굴을 들고 다닐 수가 없어요.
B: 아니, 네 언니는 왜 그러니?

얼굴을 찌푸리다
to frown

This expression can be used interchangeably with **얼굴을 찡그리다**.

ex A: 무슨 일 있어요? 왜 얼굴을 찌푸리고 있어요?
B: 지하에 있다가 밖으로 나오니 햇살이 너무 강해서요.

얼굴이 뜨겁다
one's face is hot

This is used when a person's face is flushed with fever or burning with shame or embarrassment.

ex A: 수료식에서 춤 공연을 한다고 했지요? 잘했어요?
B: 중간에 넘어지는 큰 실수를 해서 무대에서 내려오는데 얼굴이 뜨거워서 혼났어요.

얼굴이 두껍다
to be thick-skinned, to be brazen-faced

This indicates a person who is shameless.

ex A: 영수가 오늘도 또 늦나 봐. 우리끼리 먼저 발표 준비를 시작하자.
B: 매번 늦으면서 미안하단 말도 없고. 영수는 정말 얼굴이 두꺼운 것 같아.

얼굴이 피다
to have one's complexion bloom

This indicates that a person looks happy and healthier than before.

ex A: 그동안 계속 우울해 보이더니 요즘 얼굴이 좀 피었어요.
B: 지난주에 부모님이 한국에 오셨거든요. 오랜만에 부모님과 있으니까 기분이 좋아서 그런가 봐요.

얼굴이 팔리다
to be widely known

This indicates that a person becomes widely known and gains fame.

ex A: 연예인들은 왜 항상 선글라스를 쓰고 다닐까요?
B: 얼굴이 팔려서 사람들이 많이 알아보는 게 싫어서 그러는 거 같아요.

얼굴이 반쪽이 되다
to look emaciated, to have one's cheeks sunken in

This indicates that a person looks much thinner than usual. The expression **얼굴이 반쪽이 되었다**, the past form of **얼굴이 반쪽이 되다** is often used.

ex A: 요즘 무슨 힘든 일 있었어요? 얼굴이 반쪽이 됐네요.
B: 독감에 걸려서 일주일 동안 밥도 거의 못 먹고 누워만 있었거든요.

Vocabulary Check

Part 1 준비합시다 01

- 운동 부족 lack of exercise
- 뵈다 to see
- 떨어지다 to run out of

Part 1 준비합시다 02

- 수다를 떨다 to chatter

Part 1 들어 봅시다

- 마음이 흔들리다 to have one's mind shaken
- 숲 forest, woods
- 자리를 잡다 to find a place
- 줄을 서다 to stand in a queue
- 부딪치다 to confront, to face (up to)

Part 1 말해 봅시다

- 소홀하다 to be negligent, to be careless
- 일자리 job, work, employment
- 흔하다 to be common
- 기회를 놓치다 to miss an opportunity
- 틀림없다 to be certain, to be sure
- 눈 딱 감고 믿다 to just believe in
- 다가오다 to come closer
- 실망하다 to be disappointed

Part 2 준비합시다 01

- 약속을 잡다 to make an appointment
- 알아보다 to look for
- 음식을 태우다 to burn food

Part 2 준비합시다 02

- 이왕 now that, if~ at all
- 치우다 to clear away
- 출출하다 to feel a little bit hungry

Part 2 들어 봅시다

- 강연 lecture
- 칭찬을 하다 to make a compliment
- 자랑을 하다 to brag (about)
- 부쩍 suddenly, rapidly
- 원만하다 to be amicable
- 인색하다 to be miserly
- 습관화하다 to make a habit of
- 상대방 the other party
- 릴레이 relay

Part 2 말해 봅시다

- 계약 contract, deal
- 이런저런 this and that
- 눈코 뜰 새 없다 to be extremely busy
- 그다지 not so, not very
- 외근을 나가다 to work outside the office
- 웬만하다 to be tolerable
- 도저히 at all
- 곤란하다 (something) to be difficult
- 무리한 부탁을 하다 to make an unreasonable request
- 귀찮다 to be a bother
- 오히려 rather, more of
- 제출하다 to submit, to hand in

Part 3 읽어 봅시다

- 말이 통하다 to understand each other, to speak the same language
- 무심코 unintentionally, unconsciously
- 상처를 입다 to get hurt

- 자존심이 상하다 to have one's pride hurt
- 진심 sincerity
- 의도 intention
- 침묵하다 to be silent, to say nothing
- 유형 type, category, class
- 참다 to endure, to hold back
- 말대답 retort
- 억울하다 to be unjust, to be unfair
- 소중하다 to be valuable
- 대처하다 to come up with, to handle, to respond

Part 3 어휘를 늘려 봅시다

- 떳떳하다 to be proud, to be honorable
- 청첩장 wedding invitation
- 과제 task, assignment, project

Topic Vocabulary

Interpersonal Relationships

- 발이 넓다 to have many acquaintances, to have a big network
- 인맥을 쌓다 to network, to make more personal connections
- 인간관계가 원만하다 to have good relations with people
- 사회성이 좋다 to be sociable
- 친화력이 있다 to get on well with others
- 사교적이다 to be outgoing, to be sociable
- 사교성이 있다 to be sociable, to be a good mixer
- 소통이 잘되다 to communicate well
- 불화가 생기다 to have a disagreement
- 아는 사람이 많다 to have many acquaintances, to have many connections
- 사람들과 잘 어울리다 to get along well with people, to fit in well with people
- 낯을 많이 가리다 to be very shy with strangers
- 대인기피증이 있다 to have a social phobia, to have a fear of being around people
- 대인관계를 힘들어하다 to have difficulty in interpersonal relationships
- 성격이 잘 맞다 to have the right chemistry, to be born under the same star
- 성격이 안 맞다 to be incompatible with
- 관계가 멀어지다 to have a relationship turn cool/distant
- 서먹서먹해지다 to have a relationship become awkward
- 관계를 끊다 to make a break with, to cut oneself off from
- 친구와 절교하다 to end a relationship, to be through with a friend

PART1 준비합시다 01 • –(으)ㄴ/는 척하다

p.138

Grammar Focus

–(으)ㄴ/는 척하다 means to pretend to do something while not doing it, or to pretend that something is a certain way when it is not.

Basic form	–(으)ㄴ 척하다
예쁘다	예쁜 척하다
많다	많은 척하다

Basic form	–는 척하다	–(으)ㄴ 척하다
가다	가는 척하다	간 척하다
먹다	먹는 척하다	먹은 척하다
돕다	돕는 척하다	도운 척하다
만들다	만드는 척하다	만든 척하다

ex A: 아침에 길에서 넘어졌을 때 안 아팠어요?
B: 안 아프기는요. 정말 아팠어요. 그런데 사람들이 너무 많아서 안 아픈 척했어요.

ex A: 어제 소개받은 남자는 어땠어요?
B: 너무 잘난 척을 해서 별로 마음에 안 들었어요.

ex A: 저는 한국 친구들과 이야기할 때 가끔 무슨 말인지 모르면서 알아듣는 척할 때가 있어요.
B: 저도 예전에는 자주 그랬어요. 하지만 한국어를 잘하기 위해서는 모르는 건 모른다고 이야기하고 물어보는 게 좋은 것 같아요.

ex A: 김진수 씨, 드라마에서 보니까 요리를 정말 잘하시는 것 같던데요. 실제로도 요리를 잘하시나요?
B: 아니요. 사실은 요리를 전혀 못해요. 드라마에서 그냥 음식을 만드는 척 연기한 거예요.

ex A: 여자 연예인들은 화장 안 해도 피부가 정말 좋은 거 같아요.
B: 화장을 안 하긴요. 대부분이 화장하고 안 한 척하는 거예요.

ex A: 이 기사 좀 보세요. 산에서 곰을 만났을 때 죽은 척하면 곰이 그냥 지나간대요.
B: 그래요? 혹시라도 곰을 만나면 저도 죽은 척해야겠네요.

Focus Plus

- When used with a verb –는 척하다 means to pretend to be doing something or to do something all the time when such is not the case. –(으)ㄴ 척하다 is used when one pretends to have already done something when such is not the case.

ex A: 안나 씨가 만든 음식 맛있었어요?
B: 아니요. 맛이 이상해서 먹기 힘들었어요. 그래서 먹는 척만 하고 사실은 안 먹었어요.
→ This means to pretend to eat while in fact not eating.

ex A: 안나 씨가 만든 음식 맛있었어요?
B: 아니요. 맛이 이상해서 먹기 힘들었어요. 그래서 저녁을 이미 먹은 척하고 안 먹었어요.
→ This means to pretend one has already eaten although one has not.

- When pretending one will do something when he/she has no intention of doing so, the expression used is -는 척할 것이다, not -(으)ㄹ 척하다.

  ex 나는 내일 학교에 안 가지만 가족들한테는 가는 척할 것이다. (○)
  나는 내일 학교에 안 가지만 가족들한테는 갈 척할 것이다. (×)

- Only -는 척하다 can be attached to the verb 알다.

  ex 마이클 씨는 모르는 것도 아는 척했다. (○)
  마이클 씨는 모르는 것도 안 척했다. (×)

  ex A: 아까 학교 앞에서 인사한 사람 누구예요? 안나 씨 친구예요?
  B: 아니요. 모르는 사람이에요. 그 사람이 아는 사람처럼 인사를 해서 저도 그냥 아는 척했어요.

- When attached to a noun, the same expression takes the form of -인 척하다.

  ex A: 아까 영민 씨가 한 얘기 옛날에도 들었던 이야기 아니에요?
  B: 맞아요. 그런데 영민 씨가 무안해 할 것 같아서 그냥 처음 듣는 이야기인 척했어요.

  ex A: 민수 씨는 고등학교 때도 항상 모범생이었어요?
  B: 그런 편이었지만 항상 그렇지는 않았어요. 친구들과 성인 영화를 어른인 척하고 본 적도 있어요.

- A similar expression to -(으)ㄴ/는 척하다 is -(으)ㄴ/는 체하다.

  ex A: 어제 우연히 길에서 고등학교 동창을 만났는데 나를 모르는 체해서 기분이 나빴어요.
  B: 설마요. 친구가 수진 씨를 정말 못 봤을 거예요.

  ex A: 남편한테 이번 결혼기념일에는 해외여행을 가고 싶다고 했더니 들은 체도 안 하는 거예요. 너무 속상해요.
  B: 회사일 때문에 스트레스가 많아서 그럴 거예요. 다시 한번 잘 이야기해 보세요.

Answers

① 어렸을 때 피아노 선생님이 왔는데 수업 받기 싫어서 집에 없는 척했어요.
② 어렸을 때 가끔 학교에 가기 싫으면 아픈 척하고 집에서 더 잤어요.
③ 남편이 생일 선물을 감춰 놓은 것을 봤지만 선물을 줄 때 깜짝 놀라는 척했어요.
④ 제가 약속 시간에 많이 늦었다고 남자 친구가 화를 내서 우는 척하니까 결국 남자 친구가 저에게 미안하다고 했어요.
⑤ 후배가 저에게 모르는 문제를 가르쳐 달라고 했는데 저도 모르는 문제였어요. 그래서 바쁜 척하고 나중에 가르쳐 주겠다고 했어요.

Grammar Focus

–(으)ㄴ 채로 means to perform some action in the exact state which the speaker is in after performing a previous action. It is attached to a verb. It can be used in the abbreviated form –(으)ㄴ 채.

Basic form	–(으)ㄴ 채로	Basic form	–(으)ㄴ 채로
쓰다	쓴 채로	입다	입은 채로
켜다	켠 채로	열다	연 채로
꽂다	꽂은 채로	눕다	누운 채로

ex A: 어떻게 하다가 그렇게 감기에 심하게 걸렸어요?
B: 어제 갑자기 비가 와서 우산을 안 쓴 채로 돌아다녀서 그런 것 같아요.

ex A: 머리가 젖은 채로 잠을 자면 머릿결이 나빠진대.
B: 그래? 난 그것도 모르고 자기 전에 항상 머리 감고 그냥 잤어.

ex A: 영민 씨가 정말 몸이 안 좋은가 봐요.
B: 그런 것 같아요. 아까 제가 보니까 책상에 앉은 채로 자고 있더라고요.

ex A: 마이클 씨, 바지 주머니에 손을 넣은 채로 인사를 하면 안 돼요.
B: 그래요? 그러면 아까 제가 사장님 앞에서 실수를 했네요.

ex A: 어제 여자 친구 만나서 재미있게 보냈어요?
B: 아니요. 제가 약속 시간에 30분 늦었더니 여자 친구가 저녁 먹는 동안 입을 다문 채 아무 말도 안 했어요. 정말 당황스러웠어요.

Focus Plus

- –(으)ㄴ 채로 is often attached to –아/어 놓다 (See 『이화 한국어 3-2』 Chapter 11, p.79) or –아/어 두다 (『이화 한국어 4』 Chapter 4, p.75) and used in the form –아/어 놓은 채로 or –아/어 둔 채로.

  ex A: 어제 도둑이 들었다면서요? 어쩌다 도둑이 들었어요?
  B: 제가 어제 창문을 열어 놓은 채로 나왔거든요. 도둑이 창문으로 들어온 것 같아요.

Answers

① 왕치엔 씨는 잠옷을 입은 채로 학교에 왔습니다. 학교에 올 때는 옷을 갈아입었다고 생각했기 때문입니다.

② 줄리앙 씨는 안경을 쓴 채로 세수했습니다. 안경을 아까 벗었다고 생각했기 때문입니다.

③ 마리 씨는 차에 열쇠를 둔 채로 차 문을 잠갔습니다. 그때는 열쇠를 가방에 넣었다고 생각했기 때문입니다.

④ 율리아 씨는 장갑을 낀 채로 악수했습니다. 그때는 장갑을 낀 채로 악수를 하는 것이 실례인 것을 몰랐기 때문입니다.

⑤ 하오밍 씨는 손에 휴대 전화를 든 채로 휴대 전화를 찾았습니다. 그때는 휴대 전화가 손에 있다는 것을 몰랐기 때문입니다.

p.140

Vocabulary & Expression

벌떡 일어나다

벌떡 일어나다 means ***to suddenly get up***. It indicates suddenly standing up, making large movements, from a sitting or lying down position.

ex A: 영민 씨한테 무슨 일이 생겼어요? 아까 보니까 갑자기 자리에서 벌떡 일어나 사무실 밖으로 뛰어나가던데……

B: 집에 무슨 일이 생겼나 봐요. 전화를 받고 놀라서 나갔어요.

Script

(1) Wang Qian I woke up later than usual yesterday morning. I was afraid I would be late and ran to the bus stop. In my haste I tripped over a stone and fell down. There were a lot of people around on the way to work. I had hurt my knee and it was sore, but I was so embarrassed that I pretended I was fine and got up right away. But as I was getting up I hit someone passing by. I was sorry but I ran away out of embarrassment. My face still goes red when I think about it. And it bugs me that I didn't say sorry.

(2) Jason A few days ago I mistook someone for a person I know but pretended to know him. I was on my way to school when I saw someone walking in front of me who looked like my friend. I was happy to see him and called out his name, but he didn't turn around. So I ran up to him and called him again as I hit him on the back. But he wasn't my friend. I was so embarrassed that I pretended to know him, saying, "Hey, don't you recognize me?" But today I saw that person at school. I kept my head down as I walked to the classroom but I think he saw me.

(3) Yuki In Korea, you have to shut the door when you get out of a taxi. But in Japan the taxi doors are automatic. When I first came to Korea, I caught a taxi from the airport to the dormitory. Thinking that the doors were automatic, I got out without closing the door. I had paid the fare but the taxi driver was still there. He shouted something at me, but it was when I couldn't speak Korean properly and I couldn't understand him. So I pretended not to hear him and just came inside the dormitory.

Answers

(1) ① It was not the woman's arm that turned red but her face, out of embarrassment.

(2) ② The man mistook someone for another person and ended up saying hello to him.

(3) ④ The taxi driver was unable to leave because the woman had gotten out and left the taxi door open.

Vocabulary & Expression

입에 딱 맞다

입에 딱 맞다 means ***to be very much to one's taste***. It is used to describe food that is exactly to one's liking. A similar expression is 입맛에 딱 맞다.

ex A: 제가 드린 김치는 드셔 보셨어요? 너무 맵진 않으셨어요?
B: 아니요. 맵지도 짜지도 않고 제 입에 딱 맞아요.

예의에 어긋나다

예의에 어긋나다 means ***to be impolite, to do something against good manners***. This indicates behavior that is considered to be incorrect or bad manners. A similar expression is 예의에 벗어나다.

ex A: 윗사람에게 인사할 때 모자를 쓰고 인사하는 건 예의에 어긋나는 행동이에요.
B: 그래요? 그걸 모르고 제가 실수했습니다. 죄송합니다.

ex A: 어른이 계신 집을 방문할 때는 예의에 벗어나는 행동을 하지 않도록 조심해야 해.
B: 네, 알겠습니다. 조심할게요.

Script

Lee Changho	Did you have a good time at your friend's house?
Yuki	Yes, I went there last night. But after bowing to her grandmother, I fell over backwards as I was getting up.
Lee Changho	You fell over after bowing?
Yuki	Yes. It hurt a lot but I was so embarrassed that I pretended nothing was wrong.
Lee Changho	Dont' worry about it too much. Koreans often fall when making bows. But what did you take as a gift? You worried about that a lot, didn't you?
Yuki	I bought some rice cakes. I was a bit flusterated though when her grandmother asked me why I had bothered to buy such a thing. I guess she didn't like my present.
Lee Changho	No, she didn't say that because she didn't like the present. That was a way of expressing her thanks.
Yuki	Really? I was worried that she didn't like rice cakes.
Lee Changho	I see. Anyway, how was the meal? Did you eat a lot of Korean food.
Yuki	Yes, I really ate a lot. Everything my friend's mother had cooked was delicious, just to my liking. One thing though, don't Koreans hold the bowl in their hands?
Lee Changho	No. Koreans think holding the bowl in your hands as you eat is not good manners.
Yuki	I see. I didn't know you were not supposed to hold the bowl in your hands.

Grammar Focus

-(으)ㄹ 뻔하다 means that some incident or action was likely to take place or very nearly took place but in fact did not. It is generally used to express relief that the incident did not take place. It is attached to a verb and often used with adverbs such as 하마터면, 거의, or 자칫(하면).

Basic form	-(으)ㄹ 뻔하다	Basic form	-(으)ㄹ 뻔하다
넘어지다	넘어질 뻔하다	죽다	죽을 뻔하다
잊어버리다	잊어버릴 뻔하다	울다	울 뻔하다
잊다	잊을 뻔하다	눕다	누울 뻔하다

ex A: 안나 씨, 이 우산 안나 씨 거 아니에요?
B: 맞아요. 또 잊어버릴 뻔했네요. 고마워요.

ex A: 안나 씨, 여행 잘 갔다 왔어요?
B: 말도 마세요. 저 여행 못 갈 뻔했어요. 아침에 시간을 잘못 봐서 하마터면 비행기 놓칠 뻔했어요.

ex A: 아침에 학교에 오다가 차에 치일 뻔했어. 이어폰으로 음악을 듣느라고 차가 오는 소리를 못 들었거든.
B: 정말 큰일 날 뻔했네.

ex A: 오늘 아침에 늦잠을 자는 바람에 시험 시간에 늦을 뻔했어요.
B: 그래도 늦지 않은 게 정말 다행이네요.

Focus Plus

- -(으)ㄹ 뻔하다 is often used with 았/었으면 to indicate an imagined situation which is opposite to what actually happened.

  ex A: 내일 만나는 장소가 지하철역으로 바뀐 거 알고 있지?
  B: 정말? 네가 말을 안 해 줬으면 정문 앞으로 갈 뻔했네.

- -아/어서 죽을 뻔하다 is used in colloquial speech to describe a past state in an exaggerated way.

  ex A: 주말에 한라산 등반을 했다면서요?
  B: 네. 한라산이 그렇게 높은 산인지 모르고 올라갔다가 힘들어서 죽을 뻔했어요.

Answers

오늘 늦잠을 자서 아침부터 정신이 없었다. 급하게 나오느라고 양말 신는 것도 잊고 맨발로 나왔다. 버스정류장까지 뛰어갔지만 버스를 놓쳐서 회사에 늦을 뻔했는데 마침 택시가 와서 택시를 탔다. 그런데 택시가 너무 빨리 달려서 교통사고가 날 뻔했다. 회사에 도착해서 화장실에 갔는데 바닥의 물 때문에 미끄러질 뻔했다. 그리고 점심을 먹은 후에 커피 한 잔을 들고 사무실로 가다가 복도에서 과장님과 부딪힐 뻔했다. 깜짝 놀라서 들고 있던 커피도 쏟을 뻔했다. 퇴근 후에 친구를 만나러 가다가 버스에서 잠이 들어서 내려야 할 정류장을 지나칠 뻔했다. 정신없는 하루였지만 다행히 아무 일도 일어나지 않고 무사히 보낸 하루였다.

Grammar Focus

-(으)ㄹ 테니까 indicates one's intention to do something that is the pre-condition for the content of the following clause. The speaker is generally the subject and it is attached to a verb to make a request, suggestion, or command.

Basic form	-(으)ㄹ 테니까	Basic form	-(으)ㄹ 테니까
가다	갈 테니까	짓다	지을 테니까
떠나다	떠날 테니까	만들다	만들 테니까
찾다	찾을 테니까	돕다	도울 테니까

ex A: 늦어서 미안해요. 제가 밥을 살 테니까 기분 푸세요.
B: 알았어요. 다음에는 늦으면 안 돼요.

ex A: 저, 마이클 씨, 오늘 바빠요? 제가 일이 너무 많아서 그러는데 좀 도와주실 수 있으세요?
B: 네, 그럴게요. 도와 드릴 테니까 이따가 맛있는 거나 사 주세요.

ex A: 아침부터 부엌에서 뭐 하고 있니?
B: 오늘이 엄마 생신이잖아요. 오늘 아침은 제가 준비할 테니까 엄마는 쉬고 계세요.

ex A: 경찰관 아저씨, 가방을 지하철에 놓고 내렸는데 어떡해요?
B: 걱정 마세요. 저희가 찾으면 연락드릴 테니까 여기에 성함과 연락처를 적으세요.

ex A: 선생님, 한 번 더 읽어 주세요.
B: 네. 이번에는 천천히 읽을 테니까 잘 들으세요.

ex A: 음식 준비는 다 됐으니까 이제 얼른 저녁 먹자.
B: 그래. 내가 고기를 구울 테니까 네가 상을 차려.

ex A: 앞쪽에는 자리가 하나밖에 없네.
B: 나는 뒤쪽에 앉을 테니까 네가 앞쪽에 앉아.

Focus Plus

- -(으)ㄹ 테니까, which is a precondition for the following clause and expresses one's intent to do something, is not used in relation to past action and therefore cannot be used in the form of -았/었을 테니까.

  ex 나는 밥을 먹었을 테니까 저녁은 너 혼자 먹어. (×)

- The request, suggestion or command comes before -(으)ㄹ 테니까(요). In this case, two separate sentences are used.

  ex A: 빨리 청소하자. 집이 너무 더러워.
  B: 알았어. 너는 거실을 청소해. 나는 욕실을 청소할 테니까.

- –(으)ㄹ 테니까 can also be used when one is making an almost certain guess about something. (See 『이화 한국어 2–2』 Chapter 12, p.99). In such cases it is attached to an adjective or a verb, and the speaker cannot be the subject. The past form –았/었을 테니까 can be used to indicate one's guess or assumption. When attached to a noun, the present tense is –일 테니까 and the past tense is –였/이었을 테니까.

ex A: 부산에 가서 어느 해수욕장에 갈까요?
B: 해운대에는 사람이 많을 테니까 광안리로 갑시다.

ex A: 시험 기간이라 도서관에 사람이 많을 것 같아요. 자리가 없으면 어떻게 하지요?
B: 하오밍 씨가 먼저 가서 자리를 맡아 놓았을 테니까 걱정하지 마세요.

ex A: 우리 오늘 뭐 할까요? 영화나 한 편 볼까요?
B: 오늘은 토요일이라서 요즘 인기 있는 영화는 다 매진일 테니까 영화는 평일에 보기로 해요.

ex A: 안나 씨는 마이클 잭슨을 모른대요. 그렇게 유명한 가수를 어떻게 모를 수 있어요?
B: 마이클 잭슨이 인기를 끌었을 때는 아마 안나 씨가 초등학생이었을 테니까 모를 수도 있지요.

- –(으)ㄹ 테니까 can be abbreviated to –(으)ㄹ 테니. It is also interchangeable with –(으)ㄹ 터이니까 or (으)ㄹ 터이니.

ex A: 내가 저녁을 살 테니 네가 영화표를 사면 어때?
B: 그러자. 그럼 우리 뭘 먹을까?

ex A: 영화관에 사람이 많을 테니 조금 일찍 가서 표를 사자.
B: 그럼 서둘러야겠는데.

ex A: 교수님, 이번 워크숍에서 나눠 주실 자료 다 되셨으면 제가 복사를 맡기고 오겠습니다.
B: 자료는 내가 복사를 맡길 터이니 찾아오는 걸 민수가 좀 해 줬으면 좋겠는데.

ex A: 율리아 씨 아이 돌 선물은 어떻게 하는 게 좋을까요?
B: 각자 선물을 사면 부담이 될 터이니까 함께 돈을 모아서 사면 어떨까요?

Answers

① A : 제이슨 씨, 우리 이번 주말에 뭐 할까요?
B1: 월급날이라서 제가 한턱낼 테니까 인터넷에서 맛집을 찾아 놓으세요.
B2: 제가 차를 가져갈 테니까 가고 싶은 곳을 생각해 놓으세요.

② A : 제이슨 씨, 우리 이번 주말에 뭐 할까요?
B1: 제가 멋진 저녁 식사를 대접할 테니까 우리 집으로 놀러오세요.
B2: 제가 한국 궁중 요리를 할 테니까 요리법을 출력해 주세요.

Vocabulary & Expression

가까운 사이가 되다

가까운 사이가 되다 means ***to become close (with someone)***. It indicates the forming of close or intimate relations with another person. 사이 means the relationship between people.

ex A: 한국에서 친구 많이 사귀었어요?
B: 처음에는 친구가 한 명도 없었는데 한국어를 공부하면서 여러 나라 친구들과 가까운 사이가 됐어요.

ex A: 영민 씨, 수미 씨하고는 어떤 사이에요? 꽤 가까워 보이던데요.
B: 회사 동료로서 조금 친한 것 뿐이에요. 특별한 사이는 아니에요.

Script

Yuki Hello. My name is Yuki Yamashita, and I am studying Korean language at Ewha Womans University. I would like to talk about greetings in Korean. I'm a bit nervous because I've never spoken in front of a lot of people before, but I will do my best and hope that you will listen carefully.

I have been living in a boarding house since I first came to Korea. But at first, I almost mistook the boarding house lady for a very strange person. Whenever she saw me, she asked, "Have you eaten?" I couldn't understand why she kept asking me if I'd eaten. But I always answered, "Yes. I had the kimchi jjigae that you gave us a little while ago."

But as I studied Korean, I realized that asking people if they'd eaten could be used to literally ask if they had eaten but also as a kind of greeting. And gradually I realized that the question "Have you eaten?" contained the warm feelings of Koreans. It's a greeting that is closer and more intimate than "How are you?" These days, when the boarding house lady asks me "Have you eaten?" I just smile and say, "Yes. I've had a bit to eat."

I have a suggestion. Why don't you all try saying "Have you eaten?" rather than "How are you?" when you greet someone? I'm sure it will help to bring you closer together. Thank you for listening to my presentation.

Answers

(1) ③ The woman said she was nervous because she was speaking in front of a lot of people for the first time.

(2) ③ "밥 먹었어요?" is used to really ask if someone has eaten but also as a kind of greeting.

Vocabulary & Expression

일손이 부족하다

일손이 부족하다 means ***to be short of hands.*** It indicates that there are not enough people to do the work. Similar expressions are 일손이 모자르다, 손이 부족하다, and 손이 모자르다.

ex A: 요즘 농촌에서는 일손이 부족해서 문제가 많대요.
B: 맞아요. 저희 할아버지 과수원에서도 요즘 일할 사람이 없어서 걱정이에요.

ex A: 우리 학교에서 공부하는 외국인 학생들을 모두 초대하는 잔치를 한다면서요?.
B: 네. 생각보다 준비할 게 많은데 도와줄 일손이 모자라요. 민정 씨도 시간 괜찮으면 좀 도와주실래요?

Dialogue

Julia	Hello. I moved into No. 305 recently and haven't been able to say hello till now. Please, have these rice cakes.
Neighbor	Oh, thank you. You must be from another country.
Julia	Yes. I haven't been in Korea long so I still can't speak Korean well and don't know my way around the neighborhood. I hope I can ask you for help sometimes.
Neighbor	If there's anything you want to know about the neighborhood, just ask anytime. There are a lot of facilities around here so you won't find life here uncomfortable.
Julia	Yes. By the way, is there a good place to shop for groceries nearby? I'm having a housewarming tonight and need to buy a few things. Is there some place bigger than the little supermarket in the arcade?
Neighbor	If you take the local shuttle bus in front of the apartment complex, there's a big supermarket three stops away. And every Tuesday a market opens inside the complex. Oh, it's supposed to be held today. Why don't you go in front of Building 102 and see if it's still open?
Julia	Really? I'll go right away. I noticed there's a sauna in the arcade. Is it alright?
Neighbor	It's fairly clean. But it's being renovated and will be closed till October.
Julia	I was planning to go there tomorrow. I might have wasted my time.
Neighbor	Try going next week. Since it's being renovated the facilities should be improved.
Julia	I see. Thank you. I may need your help again. Oh, and I'd like to make dinner for you one day. When you have time, I'd like to invite you over to my place.
Neighbor	Okay. Let's be friends. There's a term "neighborhood cousins." And if you're short of hands preparing for the housewarming, let me know. I'll come and help you.

Vocabulary & Expression

큰절을 올리다

큰절을 올리다 means ***to make a deep bow***. 큰절 indicates a bow made not by standing up but by getting down on one's knees and bowing so low that the head almost touches the ground. 올리다 is an honorific form of "to make" and is used in the context of making a bow or greeting or saying something to an elderly person. Related expressions include 인사를 올리다 and 세배를 올리다.

ex A: 옛날에 한국에서는 아침마다 어른들에게 큰절을 올리면서 인사를 했대요.
B: 그래요? 그럼 절대 늦잠을 잘 수 없었겠네요.

ex A: 요즘 결혼 준비로 많이 바쁘시죠?
B: 네. 결혼하기 전에 양가 친척 어른들께 인사를 올리러 다니느라 정신이 없어요.

입을 맞추다

입을 맞추다 means ***to touch lips***. It indicates a light kiss. 맞추다 is used when any part of one's body comes into contact with that of another person's.

ex A: 나라마다 인사법이 다르다고 해요.
B: 맞아요. 어떤 나라에서는 서로의 볼에 입을 맞추기도 하고 또 어떤 나라에서는 코를 맞추기도 한대요.

뒤로 물러서다

뒤로 물러서다 means ***to take a step back***. It indicates moving backwards from where one is standing.

ex (지하철 승강장에서)
A: 지하철이 올 때 너무 앞쪽에 서 있으면 위험해요. 뒤로 조금만 물러서세요.
B: 네, 알겠습니다.

Reading Guide

This passage relates an experience that made an overseas student feel the cultural differences in Korea. Read it to find out what differences the student felt in Korea and in what kind of situation. (☞『이화 한국어 3-2』 p.150)

Answers

(1) ④ Differences in greetings come not from the degree of happiness at seeing someone but from cultural differences between countries.

(2) 줄리앙 씨가 수진 씨에게 첫인사를 할 때 수진 씨가 물러선 이유는 연인처럼 자신에게 뽀뽀를 하려고 했기 때문이다.

p.153

Vocabulary Expansion

맨– is placed before a noun and indicates a state where nothing has been added.

맨손
bare hands

This means hands that have nothing on them or a state of having/owning nothing.

ex A: 우리 사장님은 맨손으로 사업을 시작해서 이젠 직원이 1,000명이 넘어요.
B: 아무것도 없이 시작해서 회사를 이렇게 키우시다니 놀라워요.

맨발
bare feet

This means feet with nothing on them.

ex A: 모래사장 위에서 맨발로 걸으니까 기분이 좋네요.
B: 그렇죠? 모래가 부드러워서 발에 닿는 느낌이 너무 좋아요.

맨몸
bare body

This means a body wearing no clothes or a state of having/owning nothing.

ex A: 그 소식 들었어요? 마이클 씨가 맨몸으로 강도를 잡았대요.
B: 그래요? 평소에 태권도를 그렇게 열심히 하더니. 정말 대단하네요.

맨입
empty mouth

This means a state where nothing has been eaten or a state where one has not paid the price for something, literally and figuratively.

ex A: 제가 지난주에도 요코 씨 숙제를 도와줬는데 오늘 또 숙제를 도와 달라네요.
B: 이번에는 맨입으로 도와주지 마세요. 커피라도 사 달라고 하세요.

맨살
bare skin

This means a state where the skin has nothing on it.

ex A: 오늘 날씨가 더울 줄 알고 스타킹을 안 신었더니 좀 춥네요.
B: 맨살 위에 반바지를 입은 거였어요? 전 당연히 스타킹을 신은 줄 알았어요.

맨밥
plain rice

This means rice without side dishes.

ex A: 외국에서 살다가 고향에 오니까 아무 반찬 없이 맨밥만 먹어도 아주 맛있어요.
B: 그렇죠? 저는 며칠 해외 출장만 갔다 와도 그래요.

맨땅
empty land

This means land that has nothing on it or the ground with no covering.

ex A: 돗자리 안 가져왔어요? 맨땅에 앉을 수는 없잖아요?
B: 깜빡하고 안 가져왔네요. 미안해요. 여기에 이 신문지라도 깔고 앉읍시다.

맨바닥
bare floor

This means a floor with no covering on it.

ex A: 어제 소설가 이인수 강연에 갔었어요? 사람이 많이 왔어요?
B: 사람이 너무 많아서 앉을 자리가 모자랐어요. 그래서 저는 맨바닥에 앉아서 들었어요.

Vocabulary Check

Part 1 준비합시다 01

- 양보하다 to yield, to compromise

Part 1 준비합시다 02

- 렌즈를 끼다 to put in contact lenses

Part 1 들어 봅시다

- 빨개지다 to grow red
- 돌에 걸리다 to trip on a stone
- 벌떡 suddenly
- 등 back
- 자동문 automatic door

Part 1 말해 봅시다

- 밥그릇 rice bowl
- 종종 from time to time
- 입에 딱 맞다 to suit one's taste
- 입에서 살살 녹다 to melt in the mouth
- 예의 manners, etiquette
- 어긋나다 to go against, to go amiss
- 양손 both hands
- 팔꿈치 elbow
- 상 table
- 대다 to put

Part 2 준비합시다 01

- 쏟다 to spill
- 부딪히다 to bump into
- 맨발 bare feet
- 버스 정류장 bus stop
- 바닥 floor, ground
- 무사히 safely

Part 2 준비합시다 02

- 맛집 famed restaurant
- 한턱내다 to buy a meal (for others)
- 대접하다 to treat someone (older, superior) to a meal
- 궁중 요리 court cuisine
- 요리법 recipe
- 출력하다 to print

Part 2 들어 봅시다

- 긴장하다 to be nervous
- 발표하다 to present, to announce
- 오해하다 to misunderstand

Part 2 말해 봅시다

- 이제야 now
- 이웃사촌 good neighbor
- 지리 geography
- 장을 보다 to do the shopping
- 이것저것 this and that
- 단지 complex, estate
- 마을버스 neighborhood shuttle bus
- 정거장 (bus) stop
- 장이 서다 to have a market held
- 일손 person to work, helping hand

Part 3 읽어 봅시다

- 얽히다 to be entangled in
- 비비다 to rub
- 불쾌하다 to feel displeased
- 에스키모 Eskimo
- 친근함 familiarity
- 가지런히 neatly
- 모으다 to gather
- 숙이다 to lower, to bend
- 큰절을 올리다 to make a deep bow

- 볼 cheek(s)
- 입을 맞추다 to kiss
- 붉히다 to go red
- 물러서다 to take a step back
- 다가가다 to approach
- 표현 방식 method of expression

Part 3 어휘를 늘려 봅시다

- 자본 capital
- 통 really, completely
- 사극 historical drama
- 무릎을 꿇다 to kneel down
- 저지르다 to commit, to do
- 용서 forgiveness
- 빌다 to pray

Topic Vocabulary

Life Overseas

- 해외에 나가다 to go overseas
- 유학을 떠나다 to go and study abroad
- 이민을 가다 to emigrate
- 해외여행을 하다 to travel overseas
- 유럽 배낭여행을 가다 to go backpacking in Europe
- 세계 일주를 하다 to travel around the world
- 해외에서 거주하다 to live overseas
- 해외로 이주하다 to move overseas
- 해외에서 취업하다 to be employed overseas
- 어학연수를 가다 to study a foreign language overseas
- 의사소통이 어렵다 to be difficult to communicate
- 모든 것이 낯설다 to find everything strange and unfamiliar
- 외국 생활에 적응하다 to adapt to life overseas
- 외국 생활에 익숙해지다 to get used to life overseas
- 다른 나라 문화를 이해하다 to understand another country's culture
- 고향을 그리워하다 to miss one's hometown/ home country
- 향수병에 걸리다 to be homesick
- 타국 생활이 힘들다 to find life in another country difficult
- 해외에 정착하다 to settle down overseas
- 국제결혼을 하다 to marry someone from another country

 p.158

Grammar Focus

-아/어 오다 shows that some action or state has continued from the past to the present, or is still ongoing. It is attached to a verb and is generally used to emphasize the process of something.

Basic form	-아/어 오다	Basic form	-아/어 오다
지내다	지내 오다	살다	살아 오다
준비하다	준비해 오다	돕다	도와 오다
키우다	키워 오다	짓다	지어 오다

ex A: 벌써 졸업이라니 시간이 정말 빨리 가네요.
B: 반 친구들하고 그동안 친하게 지내 왔는데 졸업하면 만나기 힘들 것 같아서 정말 아쉬워요.

ex A: 방학 때 친구들이랑 배낭여행을 간다면서요? 좋겠어요.
B: 네. 입학하기 전부터 생각해 온 일이라서 정말 기대가 커요.

ex A: 왜 갑자기 회사를 그만둬요? 회사에서 무슨 일 있었어요?
B: 아니요. 사실은 몇 년 전부터 사업을 하려고 준비해 오고 있었거든요.
다음 달부터 본격적으로 사업을 시작하려고요.

ex A: 어제 부모님이 고향으로 돌아가셨다면서요?
B: 네. 공항에서 부모님이랑 헤어지고 나니까 그동안 참아 온 눈물이 쏟아졌어요.

ex A: 10년 동안이나 돈이 없어서 치료를 받지 못하는 아이들을 도와 오셨다면서요?
B: 저 혼자 한 건 아니고요. 저희 봉사 단체 사람들과 함께 한 거예요.

ex A: 가장 존경하는 사람이 누구예요?
B: 저희 부모님을 가장 존경해요. 부모님은 지금까지 자식들을 위해서 정말 열심히 살아 오셨거든요.

Focus Plus

- -아/어 오다 is also used to show physical movement from one place to another after the action in the preceding clause.

ex A: 아직도 몸이 안 좋아? 이따가 내가 맛있는 것 좀 사 올까?
B: 그럼 미안한데 죽 좀 사다 줄래?

- -아/어 오다 shows the action taken by a third party directed to the speaker.

ex A: 영민 씨가 갑자기 주말에 뭐 하냐고 문자 메시지를 보내 왔어요.
B: 어머, 그래요? 아무래도 영민 씨가 수진 씨한테 관심이 있는 것 같아요.

ex A: 남편하고는 어떻게 처음 만났어요?
B: 부산에 가는 기차 안에서 옆에 앉은 남편이 저에게 말을 걸어 왔어요.
이런저런 이야기를 하다가 서로 호감을 갖게 되었어요.

- –아/어 가다 shows that some action or state is ongoing in the present and will soon be complete or reach a certain state in the future.

  ex A: 아직도 밥 먹고 있어? 이러다가 학교에 늦겠다.
  B: 거의 다 먹어 가니까 잠깐만 기다려 줘.

  ex A: 유키 씨랑 유키 씨 남자 친구는 꼭 친남매 같아요.
  B: 그래요? 10년이나 만나서 그런지 점점 서로를 닮아 가나 봐요.

- –아/어 오다 and –아/어 가다 are similar in that both emphasize a process. But –아/어 오다 is generally used to talk about a process continuing from the past to the present while –아/어 가다 is generally used to talk about a process ongoing in the present and the near future.

  ex A: 김영민 씨가 정말 화가 많이 난 것 같아요.
  B: 제가 김영민 씨랑 5년이나 같은 부서에서 일해 왔는데 그렇게 화를 내는 건 처음 봤어요.

  ex A: 요즘 점점 더 자동차를 사는 젊은 사람들이 줄어들고 있다고 해요.
  B: 네. 앞으로도 한동안은 이런 추세가 계속돼 갈 것 같아요.

  ex A: 서른 살이 넘었는데 아직 취직도 못 하고 내 자신이 너무 한심해요.
  B: 그렇지 않아요. 아직 뭐를 해도 늦지 않은 나이에요. 살아 온 날보다 살아 갈 날들이 더 많은 나이인데 그런 생각 하지 말고 용기를 내요.

Answers

① A: 하오밍 씨는 애완동물을 키운 지 오래됐나 봐요.
B: 네, 초등학교 때부터 애완동물을 키워 왔어요.

② A: 마리 씨는 예전부터 한국 문화에 관심이 많았나 봐요.
B: 네, 대학교 때 한국 여행을 한 후부터 관심을 가져 왔어요.

③ A: 왕치엔 씨는 한국 친구에게 중국어를 가르치나 봐요.
B: 네, 지난 학기부터 친구의 중국어 공부를 도와 왔어요.

④ A: 줄리앙 씨는 취미로 사진을 찍기 시작한 지 꽤 됐나 봐요.
B: 네, 고등학교 때 처음 카메라를 산 후부터 사진을 찍어 왔어요.

⑤ A: 김수진 씨는 통역 대학원에 가려고 준비를 하나 봐요.
B: 네, 2년 전 통역사가 되기로 결심한 후부터 시험 준비를 해 왔어요.

Grammar Focus

-곤 하다 indicates an action that is repeated frequently or habitually. It is attached to a verb and used with expressions such as 자주, 종종, 가끔, or 곧잘. It can also be used in the form of -고는 하다.

Basic form	-곤 하다	Basic form	-곤 하다
사다	사곤 하다	입다	입곤 하다
오다	오곤 하다	만들다	만들곤 하다
오르다	오르곤 하다	듣다	듣곤 하다

ex A: 영민 씨는 어렸을 때 주로 뭘 하면서 놀았어요?
B: 저는 동네 친구들하고 자주 축구를 하곤 했어요.

ex A: 마리 씨는 스트레스를 어떻게 풀어요?
B: 저는 스트레스가 쌓이면 가끔 혼자 노래방에 가서 큰 소리로 노래도 부르고 춤도 추곤 해요. 그러면 스트레스가 확 풀리거든요.

ex A: 아까 발표할 때 긴장 안 됐어요? 하나도 안 떨고 잘하던데요.
B: 요즘 발표를 많이 하다 보니까 별로 긴장이 안 돼요. 하지만 저도 어렸을 때는 사람들 앞에만 서도 얼굴이 빨개지고는 했어요.

ex A: 하오밍 씨는 주말에 보통 뭐 해요?
B: 예전에는 종종 친구를 만나서 수다를 떨곤 했는데 요즘에는 피곤해서 집에서 잠만 자게 되네요.

Focus Plus

- -곤 하다 cannot be used with a verb that precludes repeated actions.

ex 영민 씨는 회사에 들어오기 전에 학교를 졸업했다. (○)
영민 씨는 회사에 들어오기 전에 학교를 졸업하곤 했다. (×)

正解

① A: 마리 씨는 한국에 오기 전에 보통 뭘 하면서 주말을 보냈어요?
B: 저는 주말이면 유학 비용을 마련하느라고 이것저것 아르바이트를 하곤 했어요.

② A: 아키라 씨는 한국에 오기 전에 보통 뭘 하면서 주말을 보냈어요?
B: 저는 맛있는 음식 먹는 것을 좋아해서 전국의 유명한 식당을 찾아 다니곤 했어요.

③ A: 줄리앙 씨는 한국에 오기 전에 보통 뭘 하면서 주말을 보냈어요?
B: 저는 축구를 좋아하는 친구들끼리 술집에 모여서 축구 경기를 관람하곤 했어요.

④ A: 율리아 씨는 한국에 오기 전에 보통 뭘 하면서 주말을 보냈어요?
B: 저는 집 근처 공원에서 가벼운 산책도 하고 한가롭게 휴일을 즐기곤 했어요.

⑤ A: 왕치엔 씨는 한국에 오기 전에 보통 뭘 하면서 주말을 보냈어요?
B: 저는 한국 영화에 빠져 있어서 새로 나온 한국 영화를 빠트리지 않고 보러 다니곤 했어요.

 p.160

Vocabulary & Expression

남몰래 기부하다

남몰래 기부하다 means ***to donate secretly***. 남몰래 means doing something without anyone else knowing about it. Similar expressions include 아무도 모르게 and 누구도 모르게.

ex A: 가수 이승우가 15년 동안 난치병에 걸린 어린이들을 남몰래 도와 왔대요?
B: 그래요? 노래만 잘하는 가수인 줄 알았는데 그런 선행도 하다니 정말 대단하네요.

Script

(1) Changho	Sujin, did you hear the news about the actor Lee Giyeong which is all over the Internet?
Sujin	Yes. They say he has donated a huge sum of money over the past five years, without anyone knowing about it.
Changho	That's right. He's still very young. It's amazing that he did such a good deed.
Sujin	That's not all. He frequently does volunteer work, even though he's so busy as an actor.
Changho	He's awesome. I want to live like that but it's not easy.
(2) Yuki	Changho, who do you respect most in the world?
Changho	The person I respect? I respect my father the most. My father was a taekwondo expert, and when he was young he traveled to many countries around the world to promote taekwondo. When I was little, I often went overseas with my father.
Yuki	Oh, I didn't know that. Your father seems really devoted to taekwondo.
Changho	Yes. I've never met anyone who loves taekwondo more than my father does.
(3) Julian	Sujin, do you know who this is in the newspaper?
Sujin	Of course. He's one of the figures most respected by young people these days. He was originally a doctor, but for the last ten years he has been running a computer company.
Julian	But why are there so many people who respect him?
Sujin	He doesn't think just about profit for himself but is famous for his efforts to contribute to society. As a doctor, he used to operate free clinics for the underprivileged, and most of the money he now makes from his computer company is used for society rather than himself.
Julian	Wow. He really deserves all that respect.

Answers

(1) ③ The man wants to be like Lee Giyeong because he has been active in making donations and doing volunteer work.

(2) ③ The man respects his father most because his father has worked hard to promote taekwondo to other countries.

(3) ③ The person the woman is talking about was originally a doctor but is now running a company.

Vocabulary & Expression

꼽다

꼽다 means ***to choose***. It indicates making a choice among several different options. It is generally used in the form of N을/를 꼽다 or N을/를 N(으)로 꼽다.

ex A: 외국 사람들은 한국 음식 중에 어떤 것을 좋아할까요?
B: 이번에 조사한 바에 따르면 불고기를 가장 좋아하는 음식으로 꼽았대요.

저는 할머니를 따라가려면 아직 멀었어요

저는 할머니를 따라가려면 아직 멀었어요 means that ***I have a long way to go before I'm as good as my grandmother***. A은/는 B을/를 따라가려면 아직 멀었다 indicates that B is much better at something than A. When A is the speaker, this expression is used to show humility, and when A is someone other than the speaker it is used to express a low opinion of that person's ability.

ex A: 수진 씨 요리 솜씨가 정말 많이 늘었는데요?
B: 아니에요. 저는 저희 어머니 솜씨를 따라가려면 아직 멀었어요.

ex A: 이번에 우리 축구팀에 들어온 신입 선수들의 실력이 많이 는 것 같지요?
B: 네, 조금 늘었어요. 하지만 선배 선수들을 따라가려면 아직 멀었어요.

Dialogue

Kim Sujin	Jason, who's this person in the photo?
Jason	The person who I respect the most and want to take after.
Kim Sujin	Really? Is it someone famous?
Jason	No, she's not someone famous. She's my grandmother.
Kim Sujin	Your grandmother? That's a bit surprising. Most people pick someone famous as the person they respect most.
Jason	You're right. But my grandmother was someone special.
Kim Sujin	Really? What kind of person was she?
Jason	My grandmother was not wealthy but she saved money and made donations and did volunteer work all her life. She is a wonderful person.
Kim Sujin	Wow! She sounds fantastic. It's not easy to help others when you're not in easy circumstances yourself. But does your grandmother still do volunteer work?
Jason	Yes. Right up till the time I came to Korea, I did volunteer work with my grandmother on the weekends.
Kim Sujin	Oh, I see. Jason, you're a great person too.
Jason	No. I have a long way to catch up to my grandmother.

Grammar Focus

-다 보면 indicates that in the course of doing something repeatedly or continually a new fact becomes known or a change in the state occurs. It is attached to a verb. It can also be used in the form of -다가 보면.

Basic form	-다 보면	Basic form	-다 보면
보다	보다 보면	줍다	줍다 보면
사다	사다 보면	듣다	듣다 보면
먹다	먹다 보면	만들다	만들다 보면

ex A: 여기에서 은행에 어떻게 가나요?
B: 이 길을 따라서 쭉 가다 보면 오른쪽에 화장품 가게가 나올 거예요.
거기에서 오른쪽으로 가면 은행이에요.

ex A: 요즘 일도 많고 인간관계도 힘들어서 회사를 그만두고 싶어요.
B: 누구나 회사 생활을 하다 보면 그런 생각이 들 때가 있어요.

ex A: 오늘이 어머니 생신이었는데 깜박했어요.
B: 바쁘게 지내다 보면 그럴 수도 있지요. 지금이라도 어머니께 전화 드리세요.

ex A: 얼마 전에 운전면허를 땄는데 주차가 너무 어려워요.
B: 걱정하지 마세요. 주차를 여러 번 하다가 보면 잘하게 될 거예요.

ex A: 처음에 한국에 와서는 김밥을 정말 좋아했는데 너무 많이 먹어서 그런지 이젠 김밥이 싫어졌어요.
B: 아무리 좋아하는 음식도 너무 자주 먹다 보면 싫어질 수 있지요.

ex A: 저는 이 노래를 듣다 보면 고향에 계신 어머니 생각이 나요.
B: 그래요? 어머니하고 자주 들었던 노래였나 봐요.

ex A: 제가 만든 음식은 왜 맛이 없을까요? 어머니가 가르쳐 주신 방법 그대로 만드는데 맛이 없어요.
B: 처음부터 잘하는 사람이 어디 있겠어요? 자꾸 만들다 보면 맛있어질 거예요.

Focus Plus

- Both -다 보면 and -다 보니(까) (See 『이화 한국어 3-2』 Chapter 12, p.105) indicate that in the course of doing something repeatedly or continually a new fact becomes known or a change in the state occurs. -다 보면 is used to express the usual outcome when a certain action is repeatedly performed. -다 보니(까) is used to express that a certain outcome is due to repeatedly performing a certain action. Therefore, the clause following -다 보면 is generally in the present tense or future tense, and the clause following -다 보니(까) is generally in the past tense.

  ex A: 공원에 어떻게 가요?
  B: 저기 보이는 큰 길을 따라가다 보면 공원이 나와요.

ex A: 공원에 어떻게 갔어요?
B: 저기 보이는 큰 길을 따라가다 보니까 공원이 나왔어요.

ex A: 저는 한국어를 공부할 때 듣기가 가장 어려워요. 어떻게 하면 듣기를 잘할 수 있을까요?
B: 매일 한국 드라마를 꾸준히 보세요. 열심히 보다 보면 한국어 듣기 실력이 좋아질 거예요.

ex A: 마리 씨는 어떻게 그렇게 한국어를 잘해요?
B: 한국 드라마를 좋아해서 매일 보다 보니까 한국어를 잘하게 됐어요.

- –다 보면 indicates that in the course of doing something repeatedly or continually a new fact becomes known or a change in the state occurs, while –고 보면 is used to indicate that a new fact is known or a change of the state occurs after performing a certain action or as a result of performing a certain action.

ex A: 저는 한국어의 'ㄹ' 발음을 정확하게 하는 게 너무 어려워요.
B: 처음에는 어려워도 자꾸 연습하다 보면 점점 더 좋아질 거예요.

ex A: 저는 서울에서 버스 타는 게 복잡하고 어려운 것 같아서 지하철만 타요.
B: 저도 처음엔 그랬는데 막상 알고 보면 그렇게 어렵지 않아요.

- To indicate that a new fact becomes known or a change in the state occurs in the course of repeatedly or continually performing the action mentioned before, 그러다 보면 or 그렇게 하다 보면 can be used.

ex A: 회사에서 스트레스를 많이 받아서 그런지 요즘 담배를 너무 많이 피워요.
B: 그러다 보면 건강이 나빠질 수 있어요. 담배를 좀 줄여 보세요.

ex A: 저는 쓰기가 너무 어려워요. 쓰기 실력이 잘 늘지 않아요.
B: 매일 한국어로 일기를 써 보세요. 그렇게 하다 보면 쓰기 실력이 조금씩 향상될 거예요.

Answers

① A: 새로 가입한 동아리 친구들과 사이가 서먹해요.
B: 친구들과 자주 어울리다 보면 금방 친해질 거예요.

② A: 하숙집 음식이 매워서 적응이 안 돼요.
B: 덜 매운 음식부터 시작해서 자꾸 먹다 보면 적응이 될 거예요.

③ A: 9개월이나 한국어를 공부했는데 생각만큼 말하기 실력이 늘지 않아요.
B: 한국 사람들과 자주 만나서 이야기하다 보면 실력이 늘 거예요.

④ A: 새로 산 휴대 전화의 기능이 복잡해서 사용하기 불편해요.
B: 사용 설명서를 보면서 기능을 하나씩 익히다 보면 편해질 거예요.

⑤ A: 신제품 개발에 대한 좋은 아이디어가 떠오르지 않아요.
B: 회의에서 동료들과 이야기를 하다 보면 떠오를 거예요.

 p.165

Grammar Focus

-(으)려다가 indicates that a certain action was going to be performed but was interrupted or changed to another action. It also indicates a stop or change in the course of a certain situation or state. -(으)려고 하다가 or -(으)려다 can also be used.

Basic form	-(으)려다가	Basic form	-(으)려다가
켜다	켜려다가	잡다	잡으려다가
자다	자려다가	돕다	도우려다가
놓다	놓으려다가	부르다	부르려다가

ex A: 졸업하고 유학 간다고 했었지?
B: 아니, 유학을 가려다가 그냥 여기에서 대학원에 진학하기로 했어.

ex A: 어제 백화점에서 산 옷을 바꿨어요?
B: 아니요, 옷을 바꾸려고 하다가 다시 입어 보니까 괜찮은 것 같아서 그냥 입으려고요.

ex A: 미나 씨는 왜 경영학을 전공으로 선택했어요?
B: 영문학을 전공하려다가 경영학이 취직이 잘된다고 해서 선택하게 됐어요.

ex A: 어제 일찍 끝났는데 뭐 했어요?
B: 친구를 만나려다 피곤해서 그냥 집에 가서 쉬었어요.

Focus Plus

- When using -(으)려다가 the subject of the preceding clause must be the same as that of the following clause.

  ex 아까 친구들하고 노래방에 갔었는데 (저는) 한국 노래를 부르려다 자신이 없어서 (저는) 그냥 팝송을 불렀어요. (○)

  ex 아까 친구들하고 노래방에 갔었는데 (친구가) 한국 노래를 부르려다 자신이 없어서 (저는) 그냥 팝송을 불렀어요. (×)

Answers

① A: 왕치엔 씨, 원피스를 산다고 했었지요? 잘 샀어요?
B: 아, 원피스를 사려다가 마음에 드는 것이 없어서 바지 정장을 샀어요.

② A: 마리 씨, 하숙집으로 이사한다고 했었지요? 이사 잘 했어요?
B: 아, 하숙집으로 이사하려다가 적당한 곳을 찾지 못해서 기숙사에서 계속 살기로 했어요.

③ A: 수진 씨, 아르바이트를 시작한다고 했었지요? 잘하고 있어요?
B: 아르바이트를 시작하려다가 공부할 시간이 부족할 것 같아서 안 하기로 했어요.

④ A: 박영민 씨, 집을 산다고 했었지요? 집 샀어요?
B: 집을 사려다가 집값이 너무 올라서 집값이 떨어질 때까지 좀 더 기다리기로 했어요.

⑤ A: 흐엉 씨, 머리를 자른다고 했었지요? 잘랐어요?
B: 머리를 자르려다가 긴 머리가 유행이라고 해서 그냥 기르기로 했어요.

Vocabulary & Expression

성공담

성공담 means ***a success story.*** –담 is attached to some nouns to indicate a story related to that noun. For example, 경험담 is a story from a certain experience, 여행담 is a story about a trip, 체험담 is the story from physical experience.

ex A: 방송국에서 일하는 학교 선배들이 취업 성공담 강연을 한다는데 같이 갈래?
B: 그래. 그렇지 않아도 나도 가려고 했어. 같이 가자.

ex A: 미국에 어학연수를 가려고 생각하고 있는데 어떤 준비를 해야 하는지 잘 모르겠어.
B: 그래? 그럼 어학연수를 다녀온 선배들의 경험담을 먼저 한번 들어 봐.

Script

TV host	Today our guest is Kim Sangjun, the man in the news who was recently picked in a survey of university students as the businessman they most admire, and whose recently published autobiography has become a bestseller. He will be telling us his success story. Hello, Mr. Kim. Thank you for taking time out of your busy schedule to appear on the show today.
Guest	Hello. Thank you for inviting me.
TV host	We have a lot of students in the studio audience today. Can you start by telling us about your student days?
Guest	My student days? Well, to tell the truth, I wasn't a very good student when I was young. I liked the piano better than studying and always played the piano by myself rather than study. I wanted to become a pianist. But when I was in high school my father's business fell into danger. I had no choice but to give up my dream of studying music in college.
TV host	Ah, is that so? It would have been hard to give up something you had dreamed of for so long. How did you overcome that time?
Guest	At first, the future certainly looked gloomy. But I thought to myself that life was bound to bring even bigger problems and I couldn't give up then. And I made up my mind to see everything in a positive light. Therefore, as soon as I graduated from high school I got a job and started to work.
TV host	I see. You overcame a difficult time in your life with a positive mindset.

Answers

(1) ② On this program the host is speaking with the guest, a man who has made news with his recent bestselling autobiography.

(2) ① The man wanted to be a pianist when he was young, but gave up his dream because of his family circumstances.

(3) ③ In the last part, the man says that he got a job, so the following content will be about his work.

Vocabulary & Expression

쏜살같이 지나가다

쏜살같이 지나가다 means ***to fly fast like an arrow***. It is used to say time flies by very quickly. 쏜살같이 is used to indicate that something is as fast as an arrow that has been shot from the bow.

ex A: 벌써 일요일 오후 5시라니 주말은 왜 이렇게 시간이 빨리 갈까?
B: 별로 한 것도 없이 쏜살같이 주말이 지나가 버렸어.

ex A: 영민 씨가 오늘 퇴근 시간이 되자마자 쏜살같이 사라져 버렸어요.
B: 여자 친구가 회사 앞에서 기다리고 있다던데 그래서 그런가 봐요.

일리가 있다

일리가 있다 means ***to be reasonable to some extent***. It indicates that something is reasonable or logical in some aspects.

ex A: 대기업이 다 좋은 건 아니야. 작은 회사에서 일하면 다양한 일을 해볼 수 있는 기회가 더 많아.
B: 듣고 보니 선배 말에도 일리가 있네요. 다시 잘 생각해 볼게요.

Script

Akira	Mari, the whole semester seemed to fly past, didn't it?
Mari	Yeah, it did. You said you were going home when this semester ended, didn't you?
Akira	Yes, that's right. I was going to go home. but I became so interested in Korean history that I decided to stay and study some more.
Mari	Oh, is that so? That's good.
Akira	You said you were going to keep studying in graduate school, didn't you?
Mari	Well, I'm seriously thinking of giving it up. I failed the entrance exam last time, and my Korean language studies are not going well.
Akira	You must be having a hard time. But you've already been studying here for a year. You can't give up now.
Mari	But since nothing is going as planned I am thinking of giving up.
Akira	I understand. But I think it's important not to give up your dreams and to do your best till the very end...
Mari	Yes, you're right...
Akira	Mari, there's a saying that failure is the mother of success. The results will be good if you work hard and don't give up. Good luck.
Mari	Yes. Your words have made me feel a bit better. I'll give it some more thought.

Vocabulary & Expression

실리다

실리다 means ***to be printed***. It indicates a piece of writing, illustration, or photograph is printed in a publication such as a newspaper or book. It is the passive form of 싣다.

ex A: 내가 쓴 글이 이번에 학교 신문에 실리게 됐어.
B: 와! 대단한데. 신문 나오면 꼭 읽어 봐야겠다.

마음을 고쳐먹다

마음을 고쳐먹다 means ***to change one's mind***. It indicates thinking differently about something or changing one's mind. A similar expression is 생각을 고쳐먹다.

ex A: 아직도 회사를 그만둘까 고민 중이야?
B: 아니요. 그동안 내 적성에 안 맞는 일을 하고 있는 것 같아 고민이 많았는데 우선 주어진 일을 열심히 한번 해 보기로 마음을 고쳐먹었어요.

패션쇼를 빛내다

패션쇼를 빛내다 means ***to make a fashion show better***. It indicates taking pains to make a fashion show better and more splendid. 빛내다 is the causative form of 빛나다 and means to make something shine brightly, but it also means to show something to its best advantage.

ex 저희 패션쇼를 빛내 주시기 위해 참석해주신 귀빈 여러분께 감사의 인사를 전합니다.

ex 바쁘신 와중에도 불구하고 오늘 언어교육원 수료식에 참석하시어 이 자리를 빛내 주신 여러분께 감사드립니다.

Reading Guide

This passage is a message sent by Sujin to her future self. Read it to find out what Sujin will be like in the future, and what efforts she made to become the person she is.
(☞『이화 한국어 3-2』 p.170)

Answers

(1) ① This person's parents are opposed to the idea of studying overseas.
(2) ② 밤낮없이 means all the time, regardless of day or night.

Vocabulary Expansion

미래가 없다
to have no future

This means there is neither hope nor any positive prospects for the future.

ex A: 새로운 기술 연구에 투자하지 않는 회사는 미래가 없기 마련입니다.
B: 맞습니다. 그래서 저희 회사도 기술 개발에 힘쓰고 있습니다.

미래가 밝다
to have a bright future

This means the future is positive and hopeful.

ex A: 왜 우리 회사에 지원하셨나요?
B: 이 회사는 좋은 기술과 인재들이 많아 미래가 밝다고 들었습니다.

미래가 어둡다
to have a gloomy future

This means the situation is hopeless with no prospects for the future.

ex A: 요즘 컴퓨터나 휴대 전화로 신문을 보는 사람들이 많아서 종이 신문의 미래가 어둡다고들 해요.
B: 맞아요. 요즘엔 지하철에서 종이 신문을 읽는 사람들이 별로 없어요.

미래를 준비하다
to prepare for the future

It indicates that one is doing something to achieve one's dreams and hopes.

ex A: 요즘 중국어까지 배우고 있다면서요? 그럼 4개 국어를 하는 거네요.
B: 미래를 준비하는 거예요. 앞으로는 무엇보다 다양한 외국어 능력이 중요한 것 같아서요.

미래가 다가오다
to have the future draw close

This means the future is approaching.

ex A: 다가오는 미래를 위해 준비하는 일 있어요?
B: 특별한 것은 없어요. 저는 미래보다는 현재의 삶이 중요하다고 생각하거든요.

미래를 꿈꾸다
to dream of the future

This means one is anticipating a bright future ahead of him/her.

ex A: 한국 청소년들은 정말 열심히 공부하는 것 같아요.
B: 맞아요. 모두들 밝은 미래를 꿈꾸면서 열심히 공부하고 있어요.

미래를 내다보다
to forecast the future

This means to forecast what will happen in the future.

ex A: 어제 드라마에서 '점을 본다'는 말을 들었는데 이게 무슨 뜻이에요?
B: 점을 본다는 것은 점쟁이가 다른 사람의 미래를 내다보고 뭐가 좋은지 또 무엇을 조심해야 하는지를 말해 주는 거예요.

미래가 불투명하다
to have an uncertain future

This means that the future is uncertain and therefore hard to predict.

ex A: 한 조사에서 대학생들에게 가장 고민이 뭔지 물어봤더니 '미래가 불투명하다'는 거래요.
B: 맞아요. 제 친구들도 대부분 앞으로 뭘 해야 할지 모르겠다고 해요.

Vocabulary Check

Part 1 준비합시다 01

• 초등학교	elementary school
• 가까이	close
• 이웃집	neighboring house
• 돌아가시다	to pass away
• 오래 하다	to do (something) for a long time
• 오래되다	to be old
• 예전	before, in the past
• 통역	interpretation
• 통역사	interpretor

Part 1 준비합시다 02

• (아버지를) 따르다	to follow/obey (one's father)
• 한가롭다	to be at leisure
• (영화에) 빠지다	to become absorbed in (a movie)
• 빠트리다	to miss

Part 1 들어 봅시다

• 인물	figure, person
• 닮다	to resemble
• 남몰래	secretly, without anyone knowing
• 경영하다	to manage
• 무료 진료소	free medical clinic

Part 1 말해 봅시다

• 넉넉하다	to be plenty, to be generous
• 양로원	nursing home
• 노숙자	homeless person
• 따라가다	to follow
• 꼽다	to pick, to select
• 당신	you (honorific form)

Part 2 준비합시다 01

• 서먹하다	to be unfamiliar
• 사용 설명서	instructions for use, manual
• 익히다	to learn
• 개발	development

Part 2 준비합시다 02

• 국물	soup, juice
• 기르다	to grow, to raise

Part 2 들어 봅시다

• 기업인	businessman, entrepreneur
• 자서전	autobiography
• 성공담	success story
• 전환점	turning point
• 좌우명	motto
• 극복하다	to overcome
• 분야	field

Part 2 말해 봅시다

• 쏜살같다	to be as fast as an arrow
• 눈 깜짝할 사이	in the blink of an eye
• 엊그제	day before yesterday
• 이제 와서	now, after waiting so long
• 성급하다	to be hasty
• 하루하루	day after day
• 언젠가	some day
• 계획대로	as planned
• 실패	failure
• 최선을 다하다	to do one's best
• 일리	some reason

Part 3 읽어 봅시다

• 멋지다	to be wonderful, to be great

• 디자이너	designer
• 실리다	to be printed (in a publication)
• 패션쇼	fashion show
• 무대	stage
• 편	side
• (마음을) 고쳐먹다	to change (one's mind)
• 견디다	to endure
• 멋	elegance, taste
• 담기다	to be filled
• 밤낮없이	all the time
• 감탄하다	to exclaim
• 힘을 얻다	to gain strength
• 도전	challenge
• 당당하다	to be confident
• 빛내다	to make (something) shine
• 열정	passion
• 정신	spirit, mentality
• 각오	resolution

Part 3 어휘를 늘려 봅시다

• 출산율	birth rate
• 감소	decrease
• 입시 학원	exam preparation institute
• 재수생	repeat student
• 유망하다	to be promising

Topic Vocabulary

Deciding One's Career

- 인생을 설계하다 to map out one's life
- 꿈을 키우다 to foster one's dream
- 꿈을 포기하다 to give up one's dream
- 꿈을 이루다 to realize one's dream
- 장래 계획을 세우다 to plan one's future
- 장래를 고민하다 to worry about one's future
- 진로 선택을 하다 to decide on a career
- 선택의 갈림길에 서다 to stand at the crossroads
- 미래가 불확실하다 to have an uncertain future
- 진로 문제로 갈등하다 to be undecided about one's career
- 직업 상담을 받다 to receive job counselling
- 적성에 맞다 to be suited to one's aptitude
- 취업 준비를 하다 to prepare for employment
- 대학에 진학하다 to go to university
- 대학원에 가다 to go to graduate school
- 창업을 하다 to open a business

Glossary

Ⓣ Textbook Ⓢ Study Guide

가까이 close Ⓣ 65, 150, 158 Ⓢ 45, 120
가득하다 to be full Ⓣ 30, 31 Ⓢ 23
가리다 to cover Ⓣ 95
가슴이 뛰다 the heart beats Ⓣ 31 Ⓢ 23
가전제품 home appliances Ⓣ 43 Ⓢ 36
가정하다 to suppose Ⓣ 58, 65, 67, 68 Ⓢ 50
가지 twigs Ⓣ 95
가지런히 neatly Ⓣ 150 Ⓢ 106
각오 resolution Ⓣ 170, 171 Ⓢ 121
갈래갈래 in pieces Ⓣ 95
감격 deep emotion Ⓣ 18 Ⓢ 11, 22
감독 director Ⓣ 26 Ⓢ 23
감소 decrease Ⓣ 173 Ⓢ 121
감탄하다 to exclaim Ⓣ 61, 62, 161, 162, 170, 171 Ⓢ 121
갑갑하다 to be tedious Ⓣ 115
강연 lecture Ⓣ 126 Ⓢ 88, 92, 105, 116
개발 development Ⓣ 164 Ⓢ 114, 119, 120
개발비 development expense Ⓣ 100 Ⓢ 78
거칠다 to be rough Ⓣ 115
건네주다 to hand over, to deliver Ⓣ 110, 111 Ⓢ 79
건축가 architect Ⓣ 80, 181 Ⓢ 64
건축상 architecture award Ⓣ 80, 181 Ⓢ 64
걸리다 to be hung Ⓣ 78, 85, 88, 89 Ⓢ 52, 53, 59, 64
(전화가) 걸리다 to have a call made Ⓣ 82, 83 Ⓢ 64
검색하다 to search Ⓣ 48, 49, 110, 111 Ⓢ 37
견디다 to endure Ⓣ 170, 187 Ⓢ 121
결근하다 to be absent from work, to stay home from work Ⓢ 15, 79
결승전 finals Ⓢ 20
결혼식을 올리다 to hold a wedding ceremony Ⓣ 18, 30 Ⓢ 11, 22
겹저고리 lined jacket Ⓣ 95
경력 사원 experienced employee Ⓢ 79
경력직으로 취직하다 to join a company as an experienced employee Ⓢ 79
경솔하다 to be careless Ⓣ 101–103 Ⓢ 70, 78
경영하다 to manage Ⓣ 160, 186 Ⓢ 120
경우 case Ⓣ 70, 124, 134, 142, 154 Ⓢ 51, 53
경쾌하다 to be cheerful Ⓣ 30 Ⓢ 22
계산대 counter Ⓣ 48, 49 Ⓢ 37
계약 contract, deal Ⓣ 127–129 Ⓢ 92
계획대로 as planned Ⓣ 169 Ⓢ 120
고객 client, customer Ⓣ 50, 99 Ⓢ 26, 68, 78
(마음을) 고쳐먹다 to change (one's mind) Ⓣ 170 Ⓢ 118, 121
고향을 그리워하다 to miss one's hometown/ home country Ⓢ 107
곤란하다 (something) to be difficult Ⓣ 128, 129 Ⓢ 92
공룡 dinosaur Ⓣ 53, 59 Ⓢ 35, 37
공연을 마치다 to end a performance Ⓢ 23
공연을 시작하다 to start a performance Ⓢ 23
공연을 준비하다 to prepare a performance Ⓢ 23
공연이 끝나다 to have a performance end Ⓢ 23
공연이 열리다 (performance) to be held Ⓣ 18 Ⓢ 11, 22
공통 commonness Ⓣ 59 Ⓢ 50
과수원 orchard Ⓢ 103
과제 task, assignment, project Ⓣ 133 Ⓢ 66, 82, 93
관객의 마음을 사로잡다 to capture the hearts of the audience Ⓢ 23
관계가 멀어지다 to have a relationship turn cool/

distant Ⓢ 93
관계를 끊다 to make a break with, to cut oneself off from Ⓢ 93
관련이 있다 to be related Ⓣ 66 Ⓢ 50
광장 square, plaza Ⓣ 155
괴팍스럽다 to be finicky Ⓣ 35
교체하다 to replace Ⓣ 40, 179 Ⓢ 36
교통사고가 나다 to have a traffic accident Ⓣ 144 Ⓢ 52, 65, 99
구내식당 office cafeteria Ⓣ 104 Ⓢ 77, 78
국물 soup, juice Ⓣ 165 Ⓢ 120
국제결혼 international marriage Ⓣ 84 Ⓢ 64, 107
국제결혼을 하다 to marry someone from another country Ⓣ 84 Ⓢ 107
굼뜨기 to be slow Ⓣ 115
궁중 요리 court cuisine Ⓣ 145 Ⓢ 101, 106
권문세도 powerful family Ⓣ 35
귀 기울이다 to listen to Ⓣ 75
귀머거리 deaf person Ⓣ 75
귀빈 honored guest, VIP Ⓢ 118
귀찮다 to be a bother Ⓣ 128, 129 Ⓢ 92
그다지 not so, not very Ⓣ 128, 129 Ⓢ 92
그러므로 therefore Ⓣ 70, 71, 154 Ⓢ 51
그리다 to draw Ⓣ 26, 30, 38 Ⓢ 22
그이 that person Ⓣ 175
극복하다 to overcome Ⓣ 166, 173, 186 Ⓢ 120
근교 suburb Ⓣ 80, 181 Ⓢ 64
근무 work Ⓣ 100, 102, 106, 111 Ⓢ 78
금메달을 따다 to win a gold medal Ⓣ 18 Ⓢ 11, 22
금주 this week Ⓣ 80 Ⓢ 55, 64
긋다 to draw Ⓣ 95
기대를 하다 to expect, to anticipate Ⓣ 90 Ⓢ 62, 65
기둥 pillar, column Ⓣ 95
기르다 to grow, to raise Ⓣ 165 Ⓢ 115, 120
기억나다 to remember Ⓣ 64, 95 Ⓢ 50
기억에 남다 to remain in one's memory Ⓣ 32, 70, 86, 90–92, 140, 182 Ⓢ 62, 65
기업 enterprise, company Ⓣ 104, 153 Ⓢ 78
기업인 businessman, entrepreneur Ⓣ 166, 186 Ⓢ 120
기울다 to lean Ⓣ 95
기회를 놓치다 to miss an opportunity Ⓣ 122, 123 Ⓢ 84, 92
긴장하다 to be nervous Ⓣ 146 Ⓢ 106
길몽 lucky/good dream Ⓣ 70, 71 Ⓢ 51
깁스 cast Ⓣ 65 Ⓢ 45, 49, 50
까다롭다 to be fussy, to be fastidious Ⓣ 99 Ⓢ 68, 78
깎다 to carve Ⓣ 115
깔리다 to be spread Ⓣ 85 Ⓢ 59, 64
깜짝 결혼식 surprise wedding ceremony Ⓣ 30 Ⓢ 22
깨엿 sesame taffy Ⓣ 55
깨지다 to be broken Ⓣ 38, 40, 82, 83, 88, 89, 179 Ⓢ 36
꺼지다 to be turned off Ⓣ 38, 40, 43, 82, 83, 85, 90, 179 Ⓢ 24, 28, 36, 59
꺾이다 to be broken, to be snapped Ⓣ 95
꼽다 to pick, to select Ⓣ 154, 163 Ⓢ 112, 120
꽂다 to put Ⓣ 43, 79, 110 Ⓢ 36, 54, 96
꽂히다 to be put Ⓣ 85, 88, 90 Ⓢ 53, 59, 64
꽃묶음 bunch of flowers Ⓣ 95
꽃봉오리 flower bud Ⓣ 75
꾸벅꾸벅 drowsily Ⓣ 44 Ⓢ 30, 36

대단하다 to be incredible Ⓣ 62, 63, 162, 163, 178, 186 Ⓢ 17, 20, 50, 105, 111, 118

대사 lines, dialogue Ⓣ 30 Ⓢ 22

대인 관계 interpersonal relationships Ⓣ 106, 114, 126 Ⓢ 78, 88

대인관계를 힘들어하다 to have difficulty in interpersonal relationships Ⓢ 93

대인기피증이 있다 to have a social phobia, to have a fear of being around people Ⓢ 93

대접하다 to treat someone (older, superior etc.) to a meal Ⓣ 145, 148, 149 Ⓢ 101, 106

대책 measure Ⓣ 101, 103 Ⓢ 37, 78

대처 management, handling Ⓣ 41, 43 Ⓢ 36

대처하다 to come up with, to handle Ⓣ 41, 131 Ⓢ 93

대표적 representative Ⓣ 70, 80, 181 Ⓢ 64

대학에 진학하다 to go to university Ⓢ 121

대학원에 가다 to go to graduate school Ⓢ 109, 121

대회 competition, contest Ⓣ 68, 69 Ⓢ 20, 50

덧세우다 to stand something on top of/next to Ⓣ 95

도둑맞다 to have (a thing) stolen Ⓣ 87, 89 Ⓢ 61, 65

도둑을 잡다 to catch a thief Ⓢ 52, 65

도둑이 들다 to get robbed Ⓣ 87, 89 Ⓢ 65, 96

도로 road Ⓣ 99 Ⓢ 68, 78

도망가다 to run away Ⓣ 78 Ⓢ 53, 64

도저히 at all Ⓣ 103, 128, 129 Ⓢ 89, 92

도전 challenge Ⓣ 170, 171, 187 Ⓢ 121

돋다 to grow, to come out Ⓣ 175

돌아가시다 to pass away Ⓣ 158 Ⓢ 120

돌에 걸리다 to trip on a stone Ⓣ 140, 184 Ⓢ 82, 106

돗자리 (outdoor) mat Ⓢ 105

두드리다 to knock Ⓣ 179 Ⓢ 23, 29

드물다 to be rare, to be unusual Ⓣ 99 Ⓢ 78

들리다 to be heard Ⓣ 78, 81–83, 181, 182 Ⓢ 24, 52, 53, 64

들어서다 to enter Ⓣ 95

등 back Ⓣ 140, 185 Ⓢ 106

등반 climbing Ⓢ 99

디디다 to take a step Ⓣ 110, 111 Ⓢ 79

디자이너 designer Ⓣ 170, 171, 187 Ⓢ 121

따라가다 to follow, to catch up with Ⓣ 162, 163 Ⓢ 112, 114, 120

(아버지를) 따르다 to follow/obey (one's father) Ⓣ 159, 186 Ⓢ 120

딱 just, perfectly Ⓣ 22, 23, 122, 123, 142, 143 Ⓢ 22, 85, 92, 98, 106

때우다 to eat something light Ⓣ 28, 29 Ⓢ 19, 22

떨어지다 to run out of Ⓣ 118 Ⓢ 28, 80, 81, 92

떳떳하다 to be honorable Ⓣ 133 Ⓢ 93

뛰어나다 to excel (in) Ⓣ 26, 160, 181 Ⓢ 22

뜨뜻미지근하다 to be tepid (in character) Ⓣ 35

뜯어보다 to open (and see) Ⓣ 50 Ⓢ 37

렌즈 lens Ⓣ 40, 179 Ⓢ 36, 106

렌즈를 끼다 to put in contact lenses Ⓣ 139 Ⓢ 106

로봇 robot Ⓣ 59, 63 Ⓢ 35, 38, 50

릴레이 relay Ⓣ 126 Ⓢ 92

마냥 endlessly Ⓣ 115

마련하다 to prepare Ⓣ 62, 63, 159 Ⓢ 50, 110

마을버스 neighborhood shuttle bus Ⓣ 149 Ⓢ 106

마음이 흔들리다 to have one's mind shaken Ⓣ 120 Ⓢ 83, 92

마케팅 marketing Ⓣ 104 Ⓢ 72, 78

막을 내리다 to lower the curtain Ⓢ 23

미루다 to put off, to postpone Ⓣ 41–43, 124 Ⓢ 25, 36

미혼 unmarried, single Ⓣ 110, 111 Ⓢ 78

바닥 floor, ground Ⓣ 38, 40, 80, 88, 89, 144, 153, 179, 181 Ⓢ 25, 73, 99, 105, 106

반드시 certainly, surely Ⓣ 28, 29 Ⓢ 22, 26

반벙어리 half mute Ⓣ 75

반송하다 to send back Ⓣ 50, 51 Ⓢ 37

발걸음 footsteps Ⓣ 30, 31 Ⓢ 20, 23

발명품 invention Ⓣ 53 Ⓢ 35, 37

발생하다 to happen, to occur Ⓢ 37

발이 넓다 to have many acquaintances, to have a big network Ⓢ 93

발자국 footprint Ⓣ 53 Ⓢ 35, 37

발전하다 to develop, to progress Ⓢ 51

발표자 speaker Ⓣ 103 Ⓢ 78

발표하다 to present, to announce Ⓣ 53, 146, 185 Ⓢ 106, 110

밤낮없이 all the time Ⓣ 170, 171 Ⓢ 118, 121

밤을 새우다 to stay up all night Ⓣ 81, 83, 133 Ⓢ 64

밥그릇 rice bowl Ⓣ 141–143 Ⓢ 106

방망이 wooden club Ⓣ 115

방송국 broadcasting station Ⓢ 10, 116

배꼽시계 belly clock Ⓣ 110, 111 Ⓢ 79

백호 white tiger Ⓣ 66, 181 Ⓢ 50

버럭 suddenly Ⓣ 115

버스 정류장 bus stop Ⓣ 144 Ⓢ 106

벌금 fine Ⓢ 60

벌떡 suddenly Ⓣ 140, 184 Ⓢ 97, 106

벌어지다 to take place, to occur Ⓣ 23, 30, 31, Ⓢ 22

범인을 잡다 to catch a criminal Ⓢ 65

범인을 쫓다 to pursue/chase a criminal Ⓢ 65

변성기 break of voice Ⓣ 67–69 Ⓢ 50

보관하다 to keep Ⓣ 46, 49, 179 Ⓢ 36

보람 worthiness Ⓣ 35 Ⓢ 63

보육 childcare, day care Ⓣ 100, 183 Ⓢ 78

복권 lottery Ⓣ 25, 61–63, 70, 73 Ⓢ 17, 22, 38, 42, 46

복권에 당첨되다 to win the lottery Ⓣ 26, 61–63 Ⓢ 17, 38, 42

복도 hallway, aisle Ⓣ 83, 144 Ⓢ 64, 99

볼 cheek(s) Ⓣ 150, 151, 185 Ⓢ 107

뵈다 to see Ⓣ 118, 148 Ⓢ 80, 92

부딪치다 to confront, to face (up to) Ⓣ 120, 130 Ⓢ 92

부딪히다 to bump into Ⓣ 144 Ⓢ 65, 99, 106

부서 department, division Ⓣ 104 Ⓢ 72, 78, 109

부서지다 to be broken Ⓣ 38 Ⓢ 24, 25, 36

부쩍 suddenly, rapidly Ⓣ 126, 184 Ⓢ 88, 92

부하 subordinate Ⓣ 101, 103, 114 Ⓢ 78, 79

부하 직원 junior staff Ⓣ 101, 114 Ⓢ 79

북극 North Pole Ⓣ 60 Ⓢ 50

북극곰 polar bear Ⓣ 60, 180 Ⓢ 40, 50

북을 두드리다 to beat a drum Ⓣ 30, 31, 179 Ⓢ 23

분수 fountain Ⓣ 155

분실하다 to lose Ⓣ 39 Ⓢ 36

분야 field Ⓣ 166 Ⓢ 120

불경기 recession, economic slump Ⓣ 104 Ⓢ 78

불길하다 to be ominous Ⓣ 70, 71 Ⓢ 51

불이 나다 to have a fire break out Ⓣ 44 Ⓢ 65

불쾌하다 to feel displeased Ⓣ 150 Ⓢ 106

불행하다 to be unhappy Ⓣ 63 Ⓢ 50

불화가 생기다 to have a disagreement Ⓢ 93

붉다 to be red Ⓣ 175

붉히다 to go red Ⓣ 150, 151 Ⓢ 107

awkward Ⓢ 93
서먹하다 to be unfamiliar Ⓣ 164 Ⓢ 114, 120
선녀 fairy Ⓣ 155
선반 shelf Ⓣ 88, 89 Ⓢ 55, 65
선을 보다 to meet a prospective marriage partner Ⓣ 35
선의 good intentions Ⓣ 55
선택의 갈림길에 서다 to stand at the crossroads Ⓢ 121
선행 good deed Ⓢ 111
설문지 questionnaire, survey Ⓣ 64 Ⓢ 50
성격이 안 맞다 to be incompatible with Ⓢ 93
성격이 잘 맞다 to have the right chemistry, to be born under the same star Ⓢ 93
성공담 success story Ⓣ 166 Ⓢ 116, 120
성급하다 to be hasty Ⓣ 168, 169 Ⓢ 120
성악가 singer Ⓣ 67–69 Ⓢ 50
성향 tendency Ⓣ 64 Ⓢ 50
세계 일주를 하다 to travel around the world Ⓣ 62, 63 Ⓢ 107
세금 tax Ⓢ 75
세다 to count Ⓣ 45, 154 Ⓢ 36
세면대 sink Ⓣ 42, 43, 48 Ⓢ 36
세차 car wash Ⓣ 73 Ⓢ 51
소견 opinion Ⓣ 35
소나기 (rain) shower Ⓣ 95
소름이 끼치다 to get goose bumps Ⓣ 82, 83 Ⓢ 64
소매치기를 당하다 to have one's pocket picked Ⓢ 65
소문나다 to become well-known Ⓣ 29 Ⓢ 22
소재 material Ⓣ 31 Ⓢ 23
소중하다 to be valuable Ⓣ 75, 130, 131, 184 Ⓢ 93
소질 talent Ⓣ 69 Ⓢ 50
소통이 잘되다 to communicate well Ⓢ 93
소홀하다 to be negligent, to be careless Ⓣ 122, 123 Ⓢ 92
속삭임 whispers Ⓣ 55, 155
손짓을 하다 to wave Ⓣ 95
솜씨 skill Ⓣ 105 Ⓢ 73, 112
수다를 떨다 to chatter Ⓣ 119 Ⓢ 82, 92, 110
수당을 받다 to receive an allowance(benefits) Ⓢ 79
수수밭 sorghum field Ⓣ 95
수숫단 sorghum sheaves Ⓣ 95
숙이다 to lower, to bend Ⓣ 150, 185 Ⓢ 106
숙제를 내다 to give homework Ⓣ 39 Ⓢ 26, 36
순간 이동 teleportation Ⓣ 60, 180 Ⓢ 50
숲 forest, woods Ⓣ 120, 184 Ⓢ 92
스치다 to flash past Ⓣ 110, 111 Ⓢ 76, 79
습관화하다 to make a habit of Ⓣ 126 Ⓢ 92
승강장 platform Ⓢ 104
승진하다 to be promoted Ⓣ 98 Ⓢ 31, 78
시차 jet lag Ⓣ 99 Ⓢ 68, 78
시청하다 to watch (TV) Ⓣ 105 Ⓢ 78
신고 notification Ⓣ 87, 89 Ⓢ 65
신입 사원 new recruit Ⓣ 103 Ⓢ 78, 79
신제품 new product Ⓣ 50, 164 Ⓢ 37, 114
신호가 가다 to have the phone ring Ⓣ 82, 83 Ⓢ 64
싣다 to load, to take in Ⓣ 110, 111 Ⓢ 79, 118
실리다 to be printed (in a publication) Ⓣ 150, 170 Ⓢ 118, 121
실망하다 to be disappointed Ⓣ 50, 121, 123 Ⓢ 92
실무 work, business Ⓣ 104 Ⓢ 72, 78
실용적 functional, practical Ⓣ 80, 181 Ⓢ 64
실패 failure Ⓣ 169, 173 Ⓢ 120

자동문 automatic door Ⓣ 140, 185 Ⓢ 106
자랑을 하다 to brag (about) Ⓣ 126 Ⓢ 92
자리를 잡다 to find a place Ⓣ 120 Ⓢ 92
자본 capital Ⓣ 153 Ⓢ 107
자서전 autobiography Ⓣ 166, 186 Ⓢ 120
자제 offspring, son, daughter Ⓣ 35
자존심이 상하다 to have one's pride hurt Ⓣ 130 Ⓢ 93
자체 itself Ⓣ 30, 31 Ⓢ 23
자판 keyboard Ⓣ 40, 43, 50, 179 Ⓢ 36
잔액 balance Ⓣ 45 Ⓢ 31, 36
잠 못 들다 to be unable to sleep Ⓣ 175
잠을 설치다 to sleep fitfully Ⓣ 44 Ⓢ 30, 36
잠자코 without a word Ⓣ 95
잡히다 to be caught Ⓣ 78 Ⓢ 52, 53, 64
장래 계획을 세우다 to plan one's future Ⓢ 121
장래를 고민하다 to worry about one's future Ⓢ 121
장래희망 future dream, hopes Ⓢ 51
장만하다 to get, to buy Ⓣ 44, 62, 113 Ⓢ 30, 36
장시간 a long time Ⓢ 82
장식장 display cupboard Ⓣ 38 Ⓢ 25, 36
장식하다 to decorate Ⓣ 79 Ⓢ 54, 64
장을 보다 to do the shopping Ⓣ 149 Ⓢ 106
장이 서다 to have a market held Ⓣ 149 Ⓢ 106
잦다 to be frequent Ⓣ 99, 104 Ⓢ 68, 78
재난을 당하다 to experience a disaster Ⓢ 65
재래시장 traditional market Ⓣ 84 Ⓢ 64
재미를 더하다 to add to the fun Ⓣ 30 Ⓢ 23
재생 play Ⓣ 40, 50 Ⓢ 36
재수생 repeat student Ⓣ 173 Ⓢ 121
재질 quality of material Ⓢ 34
재촉 to urge/press someone Ⓣ 115
저금통 money box, coin bank Ⓣ 70 Ⓢ 51
저물도록 till a late hour Ⓣ 115
저지르다 to commit, to do Ⓣ 153 Ⓢ 107
적당하다 to be appropriate Ⓣ 20, 31, 126, 134, 165 Ⓢ 22, 115
적성에 맞다 to be suited to one's aptitude Ⓣ 69, 106, 109, 183 Ⓢ 121
적응하다 to adapt oneself to Ⓣ 99 Ⓢ 48, 68, 78, 107
전기세 electricity bill Ⓣ 39 Ⓢ 26, 36
전등 lamp, light Ⓣ 38, 82, 83, 88, 90, 91 Ⓢ 25, 36
전망 view Ⓢ 52
전액 total amount Ⓣ 62, 63 Ⓢ 50
전원 power supply Ⓣ 40, 42, 43 Ⓢ 24, 39
전환점 turning point Ⓣ 166 Ⓢ 120
접촉 사고가 나다 to collide with another car Ⓢ 65
정 affection Ⓣ 84, 105, 146, 185 Ⓢ 64, 73
정거장 (bus) stop Ⓣ 19, 149 Ⓢ 106
정년퇴직을 하다 to retire at the regular retirement age Ⓢ 79
정신 spirit, mentality Ⓣ 35, 119, 144, 170, 171, 187 Ⓢ 82, 99, 104, 121
정의 definition Ⓣ 71 Ⓢ 51
정장 suit, full dress Ⓣ 44, 165, 182 Ⓢ 30, 36, 115
정지시키다 to stop, to pause Ⓣ 39, 47, 49 Ⓢ 36
제값 proper price, fair price Ⓣ 22, 23, 50 Ⓢ 22, 24
제격이다 to be perfect Ⓣ 22, 23 Ⓢ 22
제기하다 to raise, to bring up Ⓣ 101–103 Ⓢ 78
제안서 proposal, memorandum Ⓣ 104 Ⓢ 78
제자리 in one's place, in the same place Ⓢ 54
제출하다 to submit, to hand in Ⓣ 104, 129 Ⓢ 56, 71, 72, 82, 92

효녀 devoted/filial/good daughter Ⓣ 63 Ⓢ 50

효도 filial duty Ⓣ 63 Ⓢ 50

휴가를 내다 to take time off Ⓣ 101, 102, 103 Ⓢ 79

휴직을 하다 to take a leave of absence Ⓢ 79

흉몽 ominous/bad dream Ⓣ 70, 71, 181 Ⓢ 51

흔들리다 to be shaken Ⓣ 80, 82, 83, 120, 181 Ⓢ 52, 64, 83, 92

흔하다 to be common Ⓣ 122, 123 Ⓢ 92

흠 flaw, defect Ⓣ 50, 51 Ⓢ 37

흠뻑 very, greatly Ⓣ 35 Ⓢ 47

흥정하다 to bargain Ⓣ 84 Ⓢ 64

흥행하다 to be a hit, to be a success Ⓣ 26, 178 Ⓢ 22

힘을 얻다 to gain strength Ⓣ 170, 171 Ⓢ 121

힘차게 powerfully, energetically Ⓣ 155

About the Authors

박진철 Park Jin Chul

이화여자대학교 언어교육원 전임강사
Full-Time Instructor of ELC, Ewha Womans University

연세대학교 한국학협동과정 박사과정
ABD. in Korean Studies, Yonsei University

이소연 Soh Yon Lee

이화여자대학교 언어교육원 강사
Instructor of ELC, Ewha Womans University

이화여자대학교 국제대학원 한국학과 한국어교육전공 석사
M.A. in Teaching Korean as a Foreign Language in Korean Studies, Ewha Womans University

이승은 Lee Seung Eun

전 이화여자대학교 언어교육원 전임강사
Former Full-Time Instructor of ELC, Ewha Womans University

이화여자대학교 국제대학원 한국학과 한국어교육전공 박사 수료
ABD. in Korean Studies, Ewha Womans University